I MET DEATH on the AVENUE ROAD BUS

A MEMOIR

Samantha Albert

PICKLE PRESS
TORONTO

Note to readers:
In some instances, people or companies portrayed in this book are
illustrative examples based solely on the author's experiences,
but they are not intended to represent a particular person or organization.
Some names and identifying details have been changed
to protect the privacy of individuals.

Cataloguing in publication information is
available from Library and Archives Canada.
ISBN 978-1-7782004-0-3 (paperback)
ISBN 978-1-7782004-1-0 (ebook)

Edited by Scott Steedman
Cover and interior design by Jennifer Lum

samanthaalbert.ca

Pickle Press, Toronto

To my mother, you are where it all begins.
To Zev, you will take it forward.
To my love Daniel, you embrace us all.

And, of course, to Love House.

Whether we are young or old, whether our skin is light or dark, whether we are man or woman, we share a common humanity and are all headed for a common destiny. That should bind us together more strongly than divisions can push us apart. So long as anything other than love governs our relationships with others, we have work to do.

When the divisions win out, we need to work hard and bring that which has been broken apart back together again.

We ought to recognize that our greatest battle is not with one another, but with our pain, our problems, and our flaws.

To be hurt yet forgive. To do wrong, but forgive yourself. To depart from this world leaving only love.

This is the reason we walk.

—WAB KINEW, *The Reason You Walk*

PROLOGUE

1.

THE LAST TIME I thought I was dying, I made pickles. I craved strong, distracting sensations like the explosions of briny vapour that would shoot up my sinuses as I leaned over pots and filled jars. I longed to see the measure of my work in rows of bright green pickles glowing behind glass, each jar exhaling a "pop" as it sealed. Perhaps the strong taste of pickles would usher me out of this world, launching my spirit with a puckery goodbye. Or my kith and kin might raise a toast to me over one of the last, precious jars.

As I drove away from my doctor's office, her news weighing heavily, the urgency felt real, and I arrived home with a wet face and a back seat overflowing with cucumbers and vinegar.

"The news is not good," the doctor had said. "There are no more medications for me to offer you. We have run out of options."

We knew each other well by then and I had grown used to her greeting me with a broad smile and affectionate eyes. On that day, though, her face wore a grim line and her eyes were dark. She looked at me straight on and took a deep breath.

"This is dire, Sam. I'm so sorry."

Over the dozen years I had been ill, she had never used the word *dire*. The word ricocheted through me. She spoke again, but only a few of her words penetrated: "about a year" and "keep you comfortable." I couldn't absorb them. I had come to expect there would always be something new for me to try when a drug stopped working, but the cupboard was finally bare.

My mother had come to support me at this appointment. She was the only other witness to the moment. I sat beside her, but I wasn't with her. I felt like Alice in Wonderland after she drank the magical potions. My head was too big, my feet too small, and I was far, far away from all that I loved, with no way to go home.

—

MY PICKLE RECIPE is an adaptation of a dilled bean recipe handed down to me by a family friend, Denise, whose memory was preserved in the flavours of the pickles and jams that were left behind in her pantry. Denise and her husband, John, had taken pity on me one jobless summer when I was twenty-two and hired me as their Girl Friday. John found excuses to take me for ice cream runs when we should have been working with the sheep or tending the garden. As Denise and I stuffed beans into jars she told me stories about my father in his youth. Every time I make these beans or pickles now, her pragmatic, sometimes acerbic voice stays with me. "Oh hell" was one of her favourite responses to unreasonable things like guests arriving on time.

At my father's funeral, her one-worded whisper of "courage" in my ear was powerful. No one had ever called upon me to be courageous before. As she approached her own death, her courage did not diminish. Perhaps it was time for me to bequeath the recipe and her voice to the next generation.

—

ONCE THE PICKLES were jarred, I started a final To-Do-Before-I-Die List. I've always found comfort in to-do lists that allow you to check off completed tasks.

1. *Make pickles* ☑

My list was not comprised of extravagant things I wanted to accomplish before I died, like seeing the Grand Canyon or eating my way through rural France. Those were the activities you dreamed about when time stretched out before you.

No, this was, literally, my last to-do list. There were wills to update and subscriptions to cancel. My name had to be removed from ownership papers. Our household depended, not only on a division of labour, but also on a division of knowledge between my husband, Daniel, and me. I made the mashed potatoes; he made the gravy. I knew the quirky bookkeeping system; he knew the investing. He took our son, Zev, rock climbing; I took Zev clothes shopping.

Practical details were a safe place to dwell. If I couldn't be there to help Daniel face the massive emotional upheaval that yawned ahead or hold him and comfort him in his grief, I could at least ensure that when I died, he would not be missing half of the knowledge necessary to keep the household from going off the rails.

Who had time to go gallivanting off to France?

—

ZEV WAS LESS than a year old when I was first diagnosed with amyloidosis, a rare and life-threatening bone marrow disorder, so my illness was woven into the backdrop of his childhood. My medications had no more emotional weight than dinosaurs or Maisy Mouse.

By the time my doctor declared the situation to be *dire*, Zev was no longer a small child. He was fourteen and in the early-adolescent, awkward, braces stage that melts your heart. The two of us sipped chocolate milkshakes and walked along the river as I prepared to have my first serious talk with him as an older child about my illness. When we sat down to rest, I told him, without fanfare, that this illness, a part of our normal for his entire life, was finally catching up with me. I told him there might be no more medication to treat it and I might have only a year. I told him I thought he was old enough to handle this news.

Zev fixed his gaze upon the water as I spoke. His face was inscrutable.

"Do you have any questions, sweetie? Do you want to talk about this?"

Zev looked at me and said, "I'm so glad you told me."

"Me too." We got up to leave, scattering the ducks that had gathered near us.

I snuck peeks at Zev as we strolled, side by side. He appeared taller, more serious, leaning toward his adulthood. He almost seemed more taken with being included in this conversation than with the news itself. I didn't look like someone who was dying, so it must have seemed more academic than real to him. I took his arm and gave it a squeeze as we wound our way home.

—

IN ADDITION TO pickles and lists, I knit a blanket for Zev as a talisman of protection. Through the wobbly stitches and uneven rows, I knotted my love into squares of wild colours. I worked late into the night, my grief sometimes intertwining with the yarn.

Then I wanted Daniel to have a blanket. We spent hours in the wool store picking out the right shades of green to make him feel like he was in a forest. It became an obsession to make blankets for everyone I loved. I could not die until I had used up all of my wool and I continually bought new wool.

———

OVER THE YEARS since my initial diagnosis, death had come to hover so many times that we jokingly referred to me as a "serial death anticipator" when no one else was around. (Black humour isn't for everyone.) So I had been to the edge before, but somehow it was only then—the time I made pickles and lists, knit myself into the lives of those I loved, and first heard my doctor use the word *dire*—that I began to realize just how solitary an experience death was. I knew my intimates were out there, loving me, supporting me, but I had to prepare to move forward without them, to cut the ties, to let go. Each separation should have been full of grief and sadness, but I felt numb most of the time.

I took my pickles and my knitting needles and went into retreat to find strength and let go of the worry. A little part of me, a part I didn't easily reveal, felt some relief at the thought of my death. All of the struggling with this illness would be over. All of the struggling with life would be over. I was inspired to start another list:

Things I No Longer Have to Do:

1. *Go to the dentist.*

2. *Squish my breasts into a mammogram machine.*

3. *Figure out what to make for dinner.*

4. *Feel guilty about not being good enough/smart enough/pretty enough/disciplined enough . . .*

As much as I loved my life, I had also spent much of it aiming for perfection and falling short, believing my imperfections were the result of a failure of character: I hadn't controlled my impulses, I lacked focus, I was lazy. Rather than admiring what was good in me, what I excelled at, the little voice in my head seemed to constantly chastise me. Finally, I had to concede that there was no possibility of perfection, only acceptance. The relief was immense, but why did I have to die to release the pressure to be better than I was?

———

THREE MONTHS AFTER my doctor's dire pronouncement, I went for another checkup with her. The results of my blood work surprised us both. My kidney function had improved. This unexpected improvement meant I was eligible for a new medication cocktail, which had previously been off the table. Within a short time, it was clear that this new combination of drugs was effective. Crisis averted, again.

Of course, we all were overjoyed. But my earlier prognosis had led me to travel closer to death than ever before, to surrender and concede. Returning to the promise of living meant rejoining the stream of the world, knowing that my physical life would become increasingly restricted and uncomfortable as my disease progressed. To my dismay, all the familiar guilt and pressure came rushing back. If I was going to live as a sick person who couldn't work or contribute much to society, what was my value? Shouldn't I be doing more with my life, being of greater use, a better person somehow? And what about all my plans and dreams? What about the life Daniel and I imagined for ourselves when we got married and when Zev was born?

How do we live the life we have, rather than the one we planned and hoped for?

I didn't have any answers and my feet dragged, but slowly, slowly, I took baby steps back into life, into the world. I took back the financial tasks from my husband. I renewed magazine subscriptions. I ate all the pickles. I used up my wool. I went to the dentist.

I haven't made it to France yet.

PART ONE

2.

3.

1

THE LAST CRIMSON streaks of daylight had long disappeared by the time the airport van turned into the University of California, Santa Cruz, in April 1992. The campus looked more like a summer camp than an educational institution. I saw long stretches of unlit wilderness, punctuated by hubs of light and activity where the university buildings were clustered. We bounced along the ring road that circled the campus with our captain, a fearless woman who swore at bad drivers and wayward pedestrians.

I was exhausted and frazzled from a long day of travelling across three different time zones. My flight from Toronto to San Francisco had left early that morning. In San Francisco, I had connected with the shuttle that would convey me the two hours to Santa Cruz.

"Okay," the driver called back, "where's everyone getting out?"

"Stevenson," called out one student. "Porter." "Library." One by one, passengers named their destinations.

"Farm and Garden," I called out. Silence.

"What was that?" asked the driver after a moment.

"Farm and Garden?" The van made a clunking noise as we slowed down for a stop sign.

"Don't know it," she said.

"I've got instructions," I said, clutching the worn paper in my hands, feeling the comfort of this tangible evidence that the Farm and Garden did exist.

"Okay, I'll look at the next stop." The driver pulled the van up to a brightly lit building with a hive of students walking, sitting, chatting and playing hacky sack. A handful of passengers tumbled out and the driver turned to me. "Okay, let's see this map."

She tugged her ear as she looked at the map from different directions, her gum cracking a rhythm. "Hmm. Well. Hmm," she scratched her nose. She handed me back the map. "Well, I've never been there before, but we should be able to find this." She started the van and it struggled forward, gathering speed on a deserted part of the ring road. I crouched by her seat and read her the directions. There were no streetlights or backlit signs in this part of campus. We had left most of the buildings behind and were a weak beacon in an inky blackness. The remaining students in the van were huddled near the back, whispering their discontent at being delayed in their arrival.

The map indicated a turn off the ring road onto what felt like a forgotten goat path. The driver didn't hesitate as she turned. Everyone in the van was silent, straining to see what was ahead, listening to the creak of the van as it hit tree roots and uneven ground, and holding on to seats and bags when the bus angled downward sharply. Finally, the headlights illuminated a gate. I ran out, read the sign and gave a thumbs up. I could hear the cheer in the van.

I started to gather the large bags that held everything I would need to live for six months. I dug in my pocket for the tip money, but moved with deliberate slowness, my heart beating fast. The black outside felt tangible and spongy, as if it might consume me if I were left alone. I looked around at the people remaining on the bus. They sat with bored faces, avoiding my eyes. The driver slammed her door and came around to help me. She grabbed the two biggest bags and marched toward the gate. I stood staring.

"C'mon! Move it. I'm not leaving you until we find someone!" she shouted back at me. I hurried after with my remaining small bags, trying not to cry from her kindness in this strange new place. Together we opened the gate and stepped through. Soon the headlights were out of view and we were swallowed again by the dark.

"Look," I said, "there's a light." We followed the light to its source, a barn with stairs up to a loft. The driver waited with the bags at the bottom while I climbed up and knocked on the door. The smiling woman who pulled open the door was wearing overalls and had long blonde hair in a ponytail. Her face was broad and friendly, like an open field of wheat.

My words rushed out, a gush of nervous excitement, "HiI'mSamanthaAlbertfromCanadaIjustarrived..." She interrupted me with her own excitement, practically jumping up and down.

"We'vebeenwaitingforyou!I'mEdie! Welcome to the Farm and Garden." She hugged me and her smile coated me in a layer of honey. I had arrived.

2

WAS IN SANTA Cruz because I wanted to change the world. When I graduated from my bachelor of environmental studies degree, I believed that I had a responsibility to do big things to help protect our planet and that only big things would make a difference. David Suzuki, Maude Barlow, Vandana Shiva and Gloria Steinem were some of the key figures in the environmental and social justice movements who were making a difference. In the upper years of my undergraduate degree, I had explored the environmental and social impacts of current agricultural practices and had somehow made the leap that I could be the one to lead the way to change. I envisioned myself as a back-to-the-lander, wearing funky print dresses and Birkenstocks while I farmed acres of land by hand (and gave birth in the fields). I would write books, speak in public and influence government policy. At the age of twenty-five, I had it figured out.

Yet I did not actually know how to grow anything, a fact that would have killed my street cred (or field cred, as the case may be). Why would farmers, most of whom had farmed all their lives and descended from generations of farmers, have listened to me, a clueless transplant from the suburbs who had read a few books? I needed help.

Thus, in 1992, I applied and was accepted to spend six months participating in the Apprenticeship in Ecological Agriculture program at the University of California, Santa Cruz (UCSC), otherwise known as the Farm and Garden. Forty of us from around the world came to live in tents, cook communal, vegetarian meals, and learn how to grow food ecologically by working fields and garden beds under the tutelage of skilled gardeners and farmers.

My lofty ambitions aside, the apprenticeship was the perfect adventure for a twenty-five-year-old university graduate trapped in a mind-numbing cubicle job. Not able to find work in my field, I had taken a position selling health insurance to Canadian snowbirds vacationing in Florida and Arizona.

"Bank card line, *bonjour!*" I chirped dozens of times a day. I was good at my job and would have floated up to a managerial position in less than a year. The increasing pay, the benefits, and the private office were seductive. But in that job, my world was shrinking, closing in on me, suffocating me. I was desperate to escape, and Santa Cruz was my exit strategy.

—

I WOKE UP in Santa Cruz feeling like Dorothy landing in the technicolour world of Oz. Having come from the last gasps of a Toronto winter, I was dumbfounded by the explosion of rich hues and tints that painted lush gardens and fields. An exploration of the gardens unearthed mysterious paths, secret hiding places and living benches upholstered in chamomile. There were strawberries in April. April! In Ontario, strawberries wouldn't be ready until June. The campus was up a mountain and you could see Monterrey Bay while eating your strawberries on the kitchen deck. My new world was golden and magical. The message plastered on the tail of the farm truck read, "Another ho-hum day in paradise."

———

I WAS EAGER to set up my tent and get myself organized. Only a few weeks earlier, my parents and I had tackled the outdoor store to pick out what would be my home for six months. The store for athletic hipsters, which had an excellent selection of gear, was crammed when we arrived. We made our way to the tents and I started imagining what would work for me. A long-haired blond man nearby hailed the salesperson.

"Hey man, can you help me over here? Thanks, yeah. I'm heading out on a twenty-day solo climb on some fourteeners up in the Rockies. Yeah," he chuckled, "it's pretty cool." His eyes wandered as he spoke, to see who was noticing him.

"So, I can't decide if I need a superlight tent with an igloo entrance in case it snows or if I should go hardcore and bring a tarp and some rope. Dude, what would you suggest?"

I listened with interest, not because he was tanned and buff—not really my type—but because I was curious as to what he would decide. If the salesperson said "tarp," I might have reconsidered my tent choice. I wanted to be hardcore. But they wandered off to look at tents farther away, so I never did get to hear which one he chose.

My mother was trying to wave down a salesperson. My dad was walking around with his hands in the back pockets of his jeans, smiling and whistling in the way that he did; happy to be there, but not really focused on the task at hand. I tried to look as if I belonged in this outdoorsy theatre, as if I knew what I was doing. But most people were like the climbing guy. There were lean cyclists debating the contours of the bike seats. Rugged hikers testing boots. Experienced adventurers trying on backpacks with weights, checking out the buckling systems—actually knowing how the buckles worked—and trying to match the bag with their particular adventure. Every activity had its own special equipment and its own secret code. There was a jostling for who could be the most badass within each activity. I didn't see one other person there with their parents. Alone, maybe I could have faked it, but with my parents along, it wasn't going to happen.

Now to be fair, my parents had made the generous offer to pay for my tent, backpack and anything else I might need for my six-month adventure in California. I could complain all I wanted about having to take them along with me to the hip outdoor store, but unless I was going to pony up the money, I would have to get over myself.

"Mom, it's okay, I know what I want." I pointed to a modest tent that I was pretty sure I could live in. I'd lived in some tiny rooms over the years at university. The salesperson who had helped the mountain climber returned to our area and my mother called him over and pointed to the tent I had picked out.

"Can someone live in a tent that size for six months?"

The salesperson looked at it, looked at me, looked again at my parents. He shrugged. "It's a personal thing."

I was not long out of my environmental studies department, where I had been basted in a culture of people trying to live virtuous lives leaning toward the ascetic. No excess. Presuming the other participants in my upcoming program would have a similar outlook, I did not want to take the chance of being considered bourgeois in comparison. I would get a tent that could hold my sleeping bag, a backpack and a duffel bag and nothing else. No excess.

My mother shrugged. My father shrugged. My choice was considerably cheaper than the one they had proposed.

"Okay," said my mom, "here's the other stuff. Let's ring it up and get out of here."

As we were gathering our things, a young couple of about eighteen or nineteen came to do tricks on the mini climbing wall nearby. I overheard the young man as he said, "I wanna get in one more session at Old Baldy before my summer job starts. My buddy gave me some crucial beta for the crux on my proj."

I sighed and followed my parents. I would never, ever, fit in here. Would I fit in at the Farm and Garden?

—

EDIE OFFERED TO help me find the best spot for my tent. I hadn't seen this part of the property yet and, as we approached, I had to stop and stare. Smack in the middle of a field was a giant teepee. Nearby there was a tent the size of small house—with rooms. I turned to Edie.

"How many people live in that teepee?"

"Oh, just one. That's Kate."

"And that other big one?"

"Just one. Neat tents, huh?"

"Yeah," I said. "Stupid, stupid, stupid," I said to myself.

I set up my tent and arranged my things. Then I rearranged them. I spent weeks rearranging over and over again, trying to make the tent work. I had thought about my stuff fitting in the tent, but I had not thought about what it would be like to have me in there *with* my stuff.

And then, happily, I was the target of an intervention. My Auntie Ellie and Uncle Jerry lived north of San Francisco and invited me up one weekend to visit. Despite trying to keep up a brave front, I let it slip that my tent was troubling.

"Sammy!" my aunt said, "we have our old canvas tent from our camping years. Why don't you take it?" I protested the appropriate number of times, but a few days later they brought the tent down to Santa Cruz and helped me set it up. It didn't matter that it had that old canvas smell, that it would be a way too heavy for an interior canoe trip, that you would never find one of these in the hip outdoor store. My pride could accept it. It was a palace.

3

ON THE FIRST day of classes, we had all gathered in the tool shed and were each given our own gleaming garden forks and spades. I'd never owned my own tools before.

"Okay," said Orin, one of our instructors. "Take your tools and prep them for use. They need to be sanded and oiled. Here are the materials." And then he disappeared. I blanched and looked around, but everyone else was already focused on their task.

I looked at the sandpaper and the tools and began rubbing randomly as if I were washing dishes. My sanding efforts seemed only to create sawdust from the paper, leaving the wood unchanged. I sighed and snuck peeks at the rest of the group, who were all hard at work with smiles and satisfied looks.

Had I been more secure I might have asked for help, but, as with the tent, I did not want to draw attention to myself. I did not want it to be known that I was the only person who didn't know how to do this simple task.

A man with hazel eyes had been watching me from across the room and I saw that he was now headed in my direction. He stopped and watched me for a while. I kept my eyes on my work, hoping he would go away. Finally, he decided it was time to say something.

"You know, if you hold the sandpaper like this, it makes the work a lot easier," he said as he showed me what to do. I growled a "thanks" at him and put my head back down to work.

"Here's someone I'm not going to like," I said to myself as I went back to the work and found that he was, frustratingly, correct.

—

THE NEXT DAY, I was on cooking rotation and was introduced to food prep for forty by my partner for the day, an experienced cook who provided leadership and guidance. My favourite part of that day was taking a box of donated kiwis and painstakingly preparing them to create a giant kiwi crumble. When it came out of the oven, hot and steaming, the kiwis jutted up through the crumble topping like emeralds.

At the end of the day, I relaxed over dinner in the noisy and crowded common room, pleased with my accomplishments. The room was soothing with gleaming wood and plentiful windows. I looked around and saw plates scraped clean and happy, chatting people. I sat back and sipped my tea. As far as I could tell, this was a warm and welcoming group.

The man with the hazel eyes was heading toward me. I looked more closely at him, feeling more generous than I had the day before and embarrassed by my defensive behaviour. He was slim and strong, with broad shoulders. His strength came from working outside, rather than from a gym. I liked it. He had a prominent nose which oversaw a clear and eager face. I had noticed him laughing earlier in the day and had seen that he laughed full-on with his mouth open like my father. He gave off a good-natured energy.

I watched him approach until he was right in front of me. He knelt down on one knee, holding up his half-eaten piece of kiwi crumble.

"My name's Daniel. Carol told me that you were the one who made dessert."

"Yes! We had a whole box of kiwis."

"Well, this is the most beautiful dessert I have ever had. Maybe it's the most beautiful dessert in the world."

With him down on one knee in front of me, I could really see his eyes; hazel eyes, flecked with gold, full of kindness and wisdom. Laugh lines that were already defined. Clear, honest eyes. I could feel a flush filling my cheeks.

"Would you consider marrying me?" he said. I laughed and said Yes.

The next evening, I carried the joke further by proposing marriage to Daniel, based on the cinnamon buns he had crafted. I mean, a man who can make cinnamon buns like that...

—

DANIEL WAS FROM Southern California but had adopted Santa Cruz as his home. He introduced me to his treasured locales on our days off: the breakwater at the beach; the cliff at the edge of the ocean that you reached by sneaking through a farmer's Brussels sprouts field; and the endless meadows on campus where you could sleep out and never meet another soul. Over tubs of Ben & Jerry's Coffee Toffee Heath Bar Crunch ice cream, we criss-crossed the city and began to criss-cross our lives. Our backgrounds—middle class, educated, Reform Jewish, loving parents—were so similar that we were familiar to each other from the start, even though he was from Southern California, U.S.A., and I was from Southern Ontario, Canada.

Best of all, with Daniel I could be fully myself, like relaxing into a warm bath. There was a rightness to our being together. He made me feel worthy of love, lovable. This was a man who loved growing things, had ridden freight trains across the country, spent a winter in a tent in the Yukon, and hated football. A man with eyes I could let myself sink into. I had never been in a relationship like this before. I was hooked.

What began as an easy and compelling friendship soon transformed into love, fuelled by the romantic setting of gardens, fields and woods, and the intense days of working and living together. We declared our love one magical night on a midnight visit to the hot springs by the ocean near Big Sur. We took the whole night to learn each other and to map out a future. Six weeks after I had the "Here's someone I'm not going to like" thought, Daniel moved into my new palatial tent with his perfect forest-green flannel sheets, the kind I would have bought for myself if I hadn't been trying so hard to be spartan. He brought his sense of humour and whimsy, his patience and his love for me clear in those addictive eyes.

—

SPRING TURNED INTO summer as we rotated through assignments to the different garden sites including the field crops, the orchard, the greenhouses and the market stand. We built giant compost piles and learned how to double-dig a garden bed to make it as fluffy as chocolate cake. On market days we rushed around cutting tiny salad green mixes and

Daniel and me at the Farm and Garden program, UC Santa Cruz

creating glorious flower bouquets to accompany the hard-core lettuces and zucchini. The work was demanding, but every time I looked up from my weeding or digging, I would spot an enormous lily or a view of the ancient rosemary tree. I might glimpse the last ripe fig hidden in the foliage or turn my head up to see a tree heavy with almost ripe tangelos. Stressful evenings keeping seedbeds wet in the heat would be rewarded with unfurling bean shoots days later. If I was lucky, Daniel would be on the same rotation as me and I might look up at the same time as him and catch his eyes across the garden. His smile made me wobbly.

When I was fortunate enough to be assigned to the cozy upper garden farther up the mountain, I would often stay on at the end of the day after the others had left, to find some solitude in a shower and a few fresh raspberries. I would walk down the mountain to the main site while the last speck of sun withdrew and the lights of Monterrey Bay were kindled before me. This was always a moment of perfection that I wanted to fix in my memory: the bay, the mountain, the beauty of the campus, and the raspberry crushed sweet in my mouth.

—

AT THE END of the six-month program, I came away knowing how to double-dig a garden bed, grow fancy salad mix and build a well-balanced compost pile. I also came away with the conviction that I did not have the courage or strength to be a farmer. Farming would not be the way I would make a difference in the world.

And I came away with Daniel. He would accompany me home to Ontario, so we could explore a life together. I was deeply in love and certain I wanted to be with this man for the rest of my life. His willingness to leave sunshine, mountains and ocean behind him told me he was sincere. We would give it a go.

PART TWO

4.

5.

4

I HAD NEVER DRIVEN a truck before we bought Matilda, a small white pickup with a bright blue cap. I loved Matilda and felt strong and competent as I steered her around Santa Cruz. When the Farm and Garden program was over, we turned Matilda south to spend a few weeks in Long Beach with Daniel's parents, Barbara and Leon. They were kind enough to hire us to do some work for them.

Barbara was a petite package of energy, intelligence and curiosity. Like a hummingbird, I rarely saw her still unless she was taking one of her amazing short naps. She welcomed me in and never was lacking in questions to which she genuinely wanted to know the answer. I knew I was being vetted, but I saw her curiosity displayed with every person she met and saw it as part of who she was.

Leon was warm and welcoming and a skilled real-estate entrepreneur. He patiently taught Daniel and me how to install toilets and trusted us to change all the toilets in a building that he owned. I felt particularly proud of that accomplishment, swaggering around with a wrench as if I could perform any plumbing-related task.

One day Barbara handed me the phone and said, "Here, meet Grandma Betty." I was too surprised to be nervous.

"Hello?"

"Hello Sam, this is Grandma Betty from Pittsburgh. How are you?" Her voice was measured and deliberate.

"Oh, I'm great, having a great time here. How are you?" I looked at Daniel and mouthed, "What do I say?" He shrugged and busied himself with the dishes. I'd never been introduced to someone like this before. Was it a test?

"Well, I'm still vertical," she said. I laughed at this with real mirth. What a brilliant answer. Little did I know that this was her stock answer and one I would hear over and over again for many years to come. I never stopped appreciating it and her other deadpan statements.

She continued on. "I'm sure Danny looks very handsome to you, but you should have seen him at his bar mitzvah. He was clean-shaven and had short hair and looked *really* handsome." I guess I was supposed to overlook the beard and shaggy hair that I loved so much.

My time in Southern California was a good opportunity to start to get to know the people who might one day become my in-laws. They were smart and hard-working and had been successful in all of their endeavours. They were also loving parents who had raised a kind and loving son.

We said goodbye with affection and headed north.

—

TORONTO WAS KITTY-CORNER across North America from California. We could have taken a direct route, which would have cut our travel time significantly. Instead, we turned north to Vancouver, so Daniel could meet my ninety-two-year-old grandmother before we settled in Ontario. Who knew if and when we would come this way again?

Our first day in Vancouver, I went to see my grandma alone. She had been in a nursing home since having had a stroke three years earlier. I had fond memories of her yearly visits to Toronto when I was a child. She would teach me card games like kalooki and casino and take me out on the bus to restaurants for grilled cheese sandwiches. After dinner, she would pull out the special metal CN tower ashtray we kept for her and smoke a solitary cigarette with elegant fingers.

As an older teenager, I would travel to visit her in Vancouver. We made the rounds to the teahouse at Stanley Park and the opera, as well as other landmarks. She would take the lead, marching ahead with an umbrella, surreptitiously used as a cane, and introducing me to everyone she knew with a proud smile: "My granddaughter, visiting all the way from Toronto!"

I have a picture of her as a younger woman; she was beautiful and grand with high cheekbones and the same full lips that several of us in the family carry. By the time Daniel was to meet her, the grandness could still be perceived but was mostly hidden by deep lines. The stroke combined with age had shrunk her and left her sometimes lost and bewildered. This was not the grandma I remembered.

"Hi Grandma, it's Sam."

"Sam?" My grandma looked puzzled. Sam had been her husband's name. I was named after him.

"Samantha. Hank's daughter."

"Oh." She still looked a little confused. I'm not sure who she thought I was. Maybe her mind was still back in the time before even my father was born. I ached to be recognized, to be known by her. I wanted her to see me.

"Grandma, I've met a really nice man named Daniel." I held her papery hand as I spoke. "I want to bring him over to meet you tomorrow. Would that be okay?" She nodded and said, "Of course, but you really need to ask Mother first." Her mind already leaping away from the present moment.

I was silent for a moment with this unexpected request. I wasn't sure if she meant my mother or her mother. "Sure, Grandma. We'll see you tomorrow."

The next morning, I found Daniel puttering in the kitchen of the house where we were staying with some friends. I went and put my arms around him.

"Watcha making?"

"Bread," he said as he worked the dough on the counter.

"Bread?" What was he thinking? We were to leave soon to see my grandma.

"For your grandma."

"For *my* grandma?!"

"Yup."

I hugged him tight and kissed him before going back to my coffee and newspaper, peeping at him over the paper from time to time and shaking my head. He was a better grandchild than I was.

We arrived at the nursing home, Daniel cradling the warm bread wrapped in a protective towel. I introduced the two of them, my only living grandparent and my shiny new love, and then got out of the way.

"I'm very pleased to meet you," said my grandma as she gazed at Daniel's face. She sat up taller in her chair. Daniel sat down beside her, passing her the package. She pulled back the towel and stared at the bread. Then she smelled it, her eyes alit with the homey fragrance which, for a moment, must have crowded out the sour smell of the nursing home. She rubbed a piece between her fingers and then took a small bite and then another. Her eyes closed and *mmms* and *aahs* escaped from her mouth.

"Isn't it good, Grandma?" I said. She opened her eyes and nodded, looking at Daniel. I sat across from them and watched as they leaned in toward each other.

"Well, Ida, I met Sam while we were both learning how to farm in California."

"You're a farmer?"

"Well, yes, I guess you could say I'm a farmer."

"I always wanted to marry a farmer!"

I stared at my grandma: my grandma of the lone, elegant cigarette; my grandma who loved theatre and opera. This same, very urban grandma had wanted to marry a farmer?

"I always wanted to wear one of those farmerettes," my grandma said. Was it the outfit or the lifestyle that attracted her?

Daniel became more animated as he shared his favourite stories. "... and I used to ride freight trains around the States with my friend Jarvis."

"You used to ride freight trains?"

"Yes," Daniel answered with some hesitation, wondering if he had overstepped my grandmother's tolerance of appropriate behaviour. One beat. Two beats. Three beats.

"I always wanted to ride freight trains!" my ninety-two-year-old grandma stated as if it was a well-known fact. I was unable to contain myself any longer. "Grandma, did you really want to ride freight trains?"

She waved me away and kept her gaze fixed on Daniel. "Tell me more."

They chatted all afternoon like old friends. My grandma nibbled on the bread with delight. She was sharp and present. There was no mention of my long-dead grandfather. Her eyes were clear. Daniel's one loaf of bread appeared to have awakened something in her. Perhaps the bread, wholly delicious and seductive, gave her a reason to want to be in the present. As we said our goodbyes, she held on to Daniel's hand a long time, reluctant to let him go.

Daniel's kindness imprinted him more deeply upon my heart. He had approached my grandmother with tenderness, ready to fully engage with her. He didn't do this to impress me, his girlfriend, but because that was who he was. I don't know if my grandma truly longed for the freedom of the rails, the openness of a country farm, or the fashion of a farmerette. Perhaps she did or, as one of my cousins suggests, perhaps she was being a gracious host and trying to make Daniel feel comfortable or affirmed. It didn't matter. I had been focusing on her decline, grieving for the woman I had known before. Daniel's conversation with my grandma reminded me that she was so much more than her infirmity and her confusion. She could appreciate fine company and good food. She had a rich interior life that allowed her to imagine an alternative personal history. This picture of my grandmother is what I would remember about her in her last few years, her deterioration only surviving as a sidebar.

This simple loaf of bread also imprinted Daniel upon my grandmother's memory. Later, when she could remember little else, I would say, "Grandma, do you remember when Daniel brought you the fresh bread?"

"Oh, yes!" she would say with pleasure. And her face would open up with the memory of that magical day.

5

DANIEL AND I made our way back to Ontario and stayed with my parents while we determined our next steps. That gave Daniel a chance to get to know my parents and meet my sisters, Lori and Shelley, and Lori's husband, Joel. One day we went to Waterloo, the city I'd been living in before I left for California. Friends had organized a potluck (we loved potlucks in environmental studies) so that I could see everyone and introduce them to Daniel. For me, the main mission in Waterloo was to introduce Daniel to Sandra.

Sandra is like a character from a novel that involves magic and woodland creatures. Magic, real magic, life magic, seems to envelop her. She has clear, blue eyes and a smile as big as a streetcar. She connects with people with all of her being but does not make demands of that connection. She is generous with her time and her heart, unknowingly leaving a trail of love in her wake.

Yet she is no ephemeral being. She is not fey or new age. She is a blacksmith and clanks hammer on metal and sweats real sweat. Her fingers are usually stained black.

Sandra and I meeting in our first year at university was lucky timing. I had had friends before starting university, but my insecurities had led me to feel that these friends couldn't *really* like me. This fear was a silent barrier that kept me from going deeper. To be honest, I didn't know deeper was even an option. Who would want a deeper friendship with me? Starting university allowed me to launch in a new place with new people. I was open to change.

Sandra and I were two of four who rented a house together in Montreal, all of us being in our first year at McGill University. I was awed by my roommates. Sandra and Freya had been tree planters. They were strong and capable and dressed like hippie lumberjacks. Natalie was a full-blown hippie who had an unbelievable record collection of 60s music and a wicked sense of humour. I felt like a clueless little girl from the suburbs.

The four of us decorated the house, cooked huge meals together and recovered from those meals while we sprawled on the couch and poked fun at Miami Vice reruns or sang Joni Mitchell and Neil Young songs.

Despite the fun we could have as a group, Sandra and I craved time alone together, to have the space and quiet to expand our relationship. The fire escape allowed us to sneak into each other's rooms when we were supposed to be studying. We wanted to continue long conversations about our histories, our insecurities and our hoped-for futures. We met in the kitchen in the middle of the night to make pancakes and cheese soufflé that we ate unhurriedly, with no fear of food or conversation being commandeered by our roommates. We were constantly discovering new things about our friendship and about relationships in general that we wanted to map out together. There was never enough time. School was a distraction from the fascinating and nurturing conversations we had.

At my parents' home in Toronto

The connection Sandra and I built was trusting and generous. It bypassed or, perhaps, transcended the insecurities that had held me back before. We weren't lovers, but the relationship held almost the same intensity as if we had been.

To connect with Sandra, heart to heart, to trust the generosity of another person, opened up to me the possibility of connecting with others that way, be they new friends, old friends or family members. This new understanding put me in a mindset such that I could appreciate the preciousness of what Daniel had to offer when I would meet him six years later; a relationship that was also based on profound, genuine connection. Had I met him when I was younger, I might have written him off as "too nice."

After my first year, I left Montreal for Waterloo and Sandra followed me a year later. We were able to keep up our connection throughout our university years. When I left Canada to go to the Farm and Garden, parting from Sandra was painful. California might as well have been the moon. Who knew when we would see each other again? We cried buckets at the airport and wrote each other mournful letters over the eight months I was gone.

But now we were to be reunited and I could introduce her to Daniel. I had spoken at length about Sandra to Daniel and warned him that this friendship was non-negotiable and that Sandra would be a big part of our lives. I had written Sandra long letters about how wonderful Daniel was. I couldn't wait for them to meet.

When we arrived in Waterloo at the party in our honour, Sandra was in conversation with someone on the couch. I pointed her out and Daniel went right over. He knelt down beside her and said, "Hi Sandra. I'm Daniel. Sam has talked about you so much. I hope that there's room in your friendship with Sam for me." Sandra laughed her big, wonderful laugh and gave him a hug.

Of course, they loved each other. Part of what I appreciated so much about Daniel was that I felt that same deep trust with him that I had felt with Sandra. Daniel made me feel worthy of love, warts and all. Sandra had taught me to believe that that was possible and to not settle for less.

Sandra would be with us for every important event and Daniel would always be as eager to see her as I was. She might leave on adventures, but she would always come back to be a part of our family.

6

DANIEL AND I were invited by Susanna, an old university friend, to live on a farm near Stratford, Ontario, a town famous for its Shakespearean theatre festival. It was also home of the Ontario Pork Congress, but that does not get as much publicity. Five of us lived together at the farm that had belonged to Susanna's grandparents. We took up hobbies. We skied in the winter and swam in the pond in the summer. We all worked in the massive vegetable garden and were welcomed into the local potluck circuit.

We also found work to keep us going while we figured out what we wanted to do with our lives. I ended up at the local health food store and Daniel tried out woodworking and milking cows before being hired by a philosopher/landscaper. I volunteered to take over the leadership in the local community garden, which was still in its infancy. And I started classes with what was then called the Taoist Tai Chi Society.

Daniel and I settled into our new environment. Love had been easy in paradise. Expansive gardens, warm weather and spare time galore had provided time and space for a budding romance. In this new life in Ontario, there were more demands on our time and energy. In the summer, we had a large garden and preserved food with a frenzy. We had jobs, we had weather (it was a lot of cold for a California boy), and we had the short days and long nights of winter. We heated the house with a wood stove and there was always wood to chop.

Particularly problematic was the fact that in the dead of winter, it wasn't easy to have much space from each other. Only a few rooms in the house were heated and it was too cold to hang out outside. No matter how much we liked our roommates, that personal space was essential. Especially for someone like Daniel who had a finite amount of social energy. When he was overwhelmed from being around people for too long, he had this way of disappearing into himself. His body might be present, but he would close himself up and travel somewhere out of reach. If he was hungry, tired or in need of exercise or a shower he went to that same place.

"Are you mad at me?" became my standard question. I equated distance with an unspoken anger or frustration.

He was always surprised and contrite but was unable to control the darkness that would overtake him if he was in one of these states. It wasn't the darkness of depression, but a darkness stemming from the fact that he was a strong introvert. He enjoyed being social, but only up to a point. Too much time with people made him retreat inside, a behaviour it took me many years to adjust to. Living in a house with five people used up all of his social energy, leaving little for me.

—

WE MARRIED IN secret the first time, in a courthouse with Susanna, her partner and Sandra as our witnesses. Daniel had a hard time with decision-making and, while he was pretty sure he wanted to marry me, he wasn't completely sure. But Matilda forced the decision. She needed local license plates, which required documentation for Daniel. Thus, we performed this legal ceremony, so he could stay in the country and obsess over the decision a little bit longer. I had been long sure about him, but I could be patient.

I wore a thrift-store paisley dress and rode in the jump seat of the truck. My wedding ring was borrowed from Sandra; her grandmother's ring, worked off her finger with some difficulty. We drove around downtown Stratford for half an hour before the ceremony until we found a ring for Daniel.

We went to the registry office and sat with other groups waiting to marry, some in formal wedding attire and others in jeans. We tried not to giggle through the ceremony. When we were done, we retreated to the local pub. We inhaled burgers and nachos with beer for our wedding meal and our roommates gave us matching sets of red long underwear as our wedding gift. We took a few snapshots.

7

ONE MORNING, MY mother called and asked that Daniel and I come to visit for the weekend. Her voice conveyed a studied nonchalance. We drove in, quiet in our worry. My parents sat us down and told us about my father's diagnosis of leukemia. Leukemia was serious, but there was a good doctor and there were treatments. My father didn't want us to fuss over him.

I didn't know how to process this whole thing. It was the first time I had had to face a big illness, or a big anything. My parents seemed calm enough, but my mother's jaw was tight and she was edgier than normal. I didn't know how scared I should be.

It was a quiet beginning. My dad received outpatient treatments and we would visit him at home. He had taken a liking to Daniel early on. He adored his daughters, but at the same time, he was ready for some more guy energy. You could tell it in the way he would pick up extra food for Daniel for his supposed manly appetite (usually I would eat it). I knew my sister's husband, Joel, liked sports, which put him in great favour with my dad. Daniel wasn't a sports guy; nevertheless, they connected. I would be helping my mother in the kitchen and would stick my head into the living room and see my dad in his favourite brown velvety chair with Daniel crouched beside him, their two heads close in together, talking away. Daniel had this knack, just like with my grandmother, of drawing out stories I had never heard before. You could see the affection between them.

As the disease and treatment progressed, my father was in hospital more often. Entering his hospital room was a foreign experience; all whiteness and machines and sickly fluorescent lights and my dad looking so shrunken. He lost his lush hair and a considerable amount of weight.

Before getting sick, my dad had rarely seemed weighed down by the world. Usually, he was happily nested in family, friends, a ball game, classical music or his car. But now things had changed. As he became sicker, the buoyancy that characterized his walk through life was diminished.

Talk of bone marrow tests and chemotherapy was incomprehensible to me. I saw no need to learn this new language for a country I had no intention of settling in. I wasn't the grown-up in the room, and I defaulted to my youngest child status. My two sisters were doctors. They were the experts. I brought my father *Far Side* cartoons and candied ginger. No one expected anything of me.

—

MY FATHER AND I left the hospital to take a walk around the block. He wore leather slippers and a deep navy bathrobe over his pajamas, giving him the debonair look of an eccentric millionaire out for a morning stroll. Only the IV cart ruined the illusion.

I don't remember how we came to be walking together. We never used to take walks; we didn't have that kind of relationship. There was deep love between us, but I didn't confide in him and he rarely shared his feelings. We liked to eat together. We would talk about politics or what I was studying. Now I was enjoying the feeling of his weight on my arm as we ambled along College Street in Toronto in the sunshine, traffic a blur beside us.

"You know, Sammy," my dad started to speak, and I turned to look at him. "The doctors have said I'm probably not going to make it."

This moment is fixed in my memory. The plush of the robe, the *thwack* of his slippers, the rattle of the IV cart. I remember the rush of tears and turning my head away so as not to upset my father. But I can't remember the moment it hit. The blow came so fast; I only remember the pain that came after. We kept walking as if everything was normal.

"But, it's okay," he continued, as if he hadn't just delivered this news that was breaking my world into pieces. "I have almost no regrets. I've had a good life with a wife I love and three beautiful daughters."

He had never said anything like that before. I had never sensed unhappiness from him, but his life had seemed unexciting to my youthful self. We were silent the rest of the walk. He had said what he needed to say, and I could not speak.

—

"WHERE'S DANIEL?" MY father asked for the twentieth time.

"He's flying back from California, Daddy. He'll be here as soon as he can." I caressed his hand.

My father's leukemia had progressed quickly. The family was gathered in the hospital room: my mother, Lori, Shelley and Joel. Daniel was the only one missing now. My father had been in a period of remission ten days earlier when

Daniel decided to head to California to connect with friends and family. My dad had relapsed two days earlier and I had come to Toronto to be with him and the rest of the family. The night before, I had hunched over in front of one of the booths in the hospital lobby, gasping into the phone through my tears.

"Come home, Daniel, come home. We need you here. It's time." I had managed to catch him the night before he was to head into the mountains for a week-long backpacking trip. Now, he would be on the first plane home. Still, California was far.

My father drifted in and out of consciousness. We had all said our individual goodbyes, but he continued to fret and call for Daniel and could not be comforted. I knew he was in pain and it was a tricky balance to keep him comfortable yet conscious. Time stretched out as we watched the hands on the clock move at a glacial pace and counted down the hours and then the minutes.

At last, it was time. Joel picked up Daniel at the airport and they came rushing into the room. Daniel sat down close to my dad and took his hand. This time when my dad said, "Where's Daniel?" Daniel was there to respond.

"Hi, Hank. It's Daniel. I'm here."

My father's face softened, and his body relaxed. We all gathered around.

"Take care of Sammy, okay?"

"Of course I will, Hank."

I could barely see the two of them through my tears.

My mother's voice came out from the dark. "Sam can take care of herself!"

Daniel kept his eyes focused on my dad and smiled. "We will look after each other."

My dad nodded, sank back on his pillow and closed his eyes. That night, we accompanied him on the slow journey out of his body until he died early the next morning, January 16, 1994.

The weather that week was the coldest we could remember as we huddled around the grave and said the prayers. My father's death represented the first major loss in my life. I hadn't understood, understood in a real-life way, that you could lose people. It seemed unimaginable that my father was no longer in this world, a world that was lonelier and scarier than it had been before.

8

ON A FRIGID February day, a few weeks after my father's death, Daniel came and joined me in the den. I was nestled in by the fire with a book, although mostly I just gazed at the fire, thinking about my father.

"Sam, I went shopping yesterday and got all this amazing food, so we could go have a picnic."

"A picnic? In February? I'll have an indoor picnic with you. Here by the fire." I turned back to the fire. But Daniel was still in the honeymoon stage of his relationship with winter and thought we should be enjoying every beautiful day outside.

"I talked to Ken, and he said we could climb his silo and have our picnic up there." Our neighbour across the concession line was a kind pig farmer who thought we were a little strange but looked out for us all the same.

"It would be like being up on a mountain. And I miss the mountains so much." He gave me one of his puppy-dog looks.

"On top of the silo?! How do we get up there?"

"There's a ladder. It will be fine."

I looked at the fire another moment, unwilling to separate myself from it. Then I looked at Daniel's excited face and laughed. "Okay, let's go."

The temperatures had often dipped below minus-twenty degrees Celsius that winter. It was the kind of cold that hurt. The kind where your nose hairs froze. The kind that could result in frostbite. We bundled up in layers of sweaters and heavy jackets. We pulled on snow pants and big warm boots. We encased our heads in hats and scarves. I felt more round than tall, as if, like a beetle, I could easily be stranded on my back, waving my legs and arms in vain. I followed Daniel across the concession line onto our neighbour's property. The "ladder" was open-air rungs sticking out from the side of the silo. I balked, but Daniel dragged me forward. He cajoled and coddled me up that ladder. My forehead kissed the concrete silo as I mastered each rung and gathered the courage to go up the next one.

When we crested the top of the ladder, the wind came howling over the roof. The tops of silos are not flat, as I had thought, but conical with a little ledge, like a pylon. I lay back on the slope and hung on with a death grip as the wind whipped away first the rose that Daniel pulled out of his backpack and then the lid of the smoked oysters he had bought for our romantic picnic. I made a valiant effort to eat, but it was hard to do so with both hands gripping the roof.

I eyed Daniel as he pulled out a little white box. Comprehension came flooding in as to the reason for this climb... on top of a silo... in February.

I was wary about the box itself. I had never been a diamond kind of gal. I wore thrift-store clothing and hand-crafted, funky earrings. I didn't want the responsibility of a diamond and I had made that fact clear to Daniel.

With a grin, Daniel opened the box and handed it to me. I inspected the ring inside and giggled.

"When I was in California, I found this beautiful shell on the beach in Santa Cruz. I brought it to this jeweller here and told the guy how to cut it and what kind of ring I wanted. I imagined a slice of shell in a tasteful setting. But when I went to pick it up, this is what they had done." Daniel looked so embarrassed I had to laugh.

I looked at the ring. It looked like a breast surrounded by exaggerated gold curlicues. Or maybe an eyeball. It was exactly the perfect ring for me. I might not actually wear it, but I would cherish it far more than any diamond.

"I really wanted to propose to you on a mountain, but, well, there are no mountains around here," Daniel told me. "But then I thought we could kind of pretend this was a mountain." It was too precarious to go down on one knee, but he managed to hold the ring up while keeping our picnic from blowing away.

I can't remember what he said, and I'm sure he had planned out a beautiful speech. But my memory of the moment is clouded by the icy wind, the pieces of our picnic flying off the roof and the sick feeling I had when I thought about the climb down. The words were not as important as knowing he was ready to commit to our relationship fully. He had finally made the decision.

I may not remember his exact words, but I do remember my response. I kissed him and said, "Yes. Of course." And then, "Can we go down now?"

—

WE HAD OUR public wedding the following August, the one with friends and family and a rabbi. My mother organized

Daniel and me on our "official" wedding day

the event through her grief. Friends of ours, Marsha and Eric, let us use their farm. We were married up on a hill, under a crazy purple and red *chuppah* or wedding canopy that Sandra had made, with little birds hanging as a fringe around the outside perimeter. Our family and friends sang us up the hill as we marched toward the *chuppah* and the service was conducted by a progressive rabbi-friend of Daniel's. The evening party was under a full moon with a bonfire, klezmer music and, for those late-night daring folks, skinny-dipping in the pond. We were launched with love on our life together.

PART THREE

6.

7.

9

JULY WOULD BE a good month to have a baby. We had worked through the calendar, considered the realities of our life and decided that it should be July 1999. My contract with a rural women's organization would be over in June. Daniel was three years into his landscaping business and had found that July and August provided enough breathing room to accommodate the time he would need to take off.

People who heard of our plan said things like, "Uh, it doesn't usually work like this." Or, "It could take months or even years before you get pregnant."

But out from among the naysayers, a coworker, Carol, came forward and said, "This is what you do. Go out and buy a dress. The tighter the better, really form-fitting. It helps if it's expensive. Make sure it's a dress you will never be able to wear again after you have been pregnant. Wear it to a party, so it's absolutely not returnable. *Then* you will get pregnant."

Whether it was luck or Carol's shamanic dress wisdom, I became pregnant the first month. Due date in July 1999. Who said we couldn't direct our future?

—

I HAD OFTEN wondered throughout my adolescence and young adulthood if I was too selfish to have children. That is, would I put my needs before those of my child? I figured if there was only one piece of bread left and we were starving, I would definitely give it to my child. But I might not save, for example, the less urgent last chocolate for my little one or let myself be disturbed from a good book to play *Candyland*.

Throughout the pregnancy, I cycled through different and often conflicting states of mind. There was the selfishness trope, which might be followed by the panic trope—was I even up for this great experiment? At the same time, deep down, I believed it was possible to be the perfect mother. I tuned my radar to that station and aimed for perfection. Perfection in a hip, understated way; not a helicopter parent. I would get the balance right.

—

ON JULY 17, 1999, a major thunderstorm raged outside. The twenty hours of labour were a blur with only brief snapshots of memory: the pacing; the moaning; the spasms of pain; the drifting in and out of consciousness. The midwife had big, beefy hands. The doctor who eventually needed to take over was kind. Daniel was terrified for me, and Sandra was there to reassure him. Mozart penetrated the pain and the fog. Finally, the prize at the end. Our son, Zev Henry Shoag. *Henry* for my father, Henry Albert. *Zev* for Daniel's grandfather, Leon's father. His name was Wolf Shoag. The Hebrew for *wolf* is *Zev*. *Shoag* because there were very few of them left in the world.

The minute Zev was laid on my chest, the whole world contracted to the trio of Daniel, Zev and me. I swam in vast and turbulent emotions fuelled by hormones and exhaustion. Daniel and I looked at each other in amazement and love. We were now a family.

Then, when I could sit up and drag my eyes away from our son, I realized I was ravenous, the way one is after passing through the fires. Zev may have been the centre, but my stomach was growling after the many hours of hard labour and not eating.

But my hunger was specific. I wanted chicken-corn pizza from a local restaurant. Maybe "want" is too weak a word. I was ready to slide out of bed and crawl on all fours through the city to fulfill the desperate longing I had for that particular pizza.

Daniel, wild-eyed and exhausted, went on the mission to seek my pizza. He walked into the crowded, noisy restaurant and put his request to the hostess, who replied,

"I'm sorry sir, but we don't do takeout."

Daniel leaned in toward the hostess, peering at her through red eyes.

"Let me explain," he said, and went on to tell her of the two days of no sleep, the twenty hours of labour, the moaning, his fears for me and, finally, the birth of our first child and my immense, specific hunger for the chicken-corn pizza from this restaurant. He leaned in closer.

"Of all the pizzas in town, this is the one my wife has asked for. I can't go back to the mother of my newborn son without this pizza in hand."

"Coming up right away, sir."

—

THE FIRST FEW months after Zev's birth were so clean and simple. My world was Zev, entirely Zev, without distraction. I was high on his sweet baby smell and could not possibly resent anything to do with his care. When Zev woke at night, I ran into his room, eager. He rarely persisted in his crying. I would sink into the rocking chair with a happy sigh. He would make those lovely *glug glug* noises and I would look out at the stoplight down the road changing through green, yellow and red for an empty street.

Sometimes in the daytime, I relaxed with a book and a snack, enjoying the enforced rest. Zev snorted through his greedy hunger and I wiped my crumbs out of his perfectly shaped ears and stared at his perfect little hands. He slept, he ate, he pooped and, little by little, he woke up to the world. I didn't need to be anywhere or do anything, and I didn't need to make any difficult decisions yet. Life felt like perfection. I was only slightly distracted from this perfection by the little lymph node that swelled up under my arm when Zev was about five months old. But then Zev would smile at me with eyes that crinkled like mine and everything else would be forgotten.

Elated to be parents

10

N O ONE HAD warned me about mother guilt, a sticky, oozy guilt that is far more concentrated and intense than all the guilt I had experienced before. It kicked in when Zev was about six months. I felt its pangs every time I picked up another package of Pampers, letting my cloth diapers gather dust. I felt it when I let Zev cry too long or when I bought jars of pre-made baby food instead of blending up beautiful, organic squash. When another mother would say, "Oh, you gave Zev supermarket cereal at six months? That's way too soon," I fell into the guilt whirlpool as if I wore cement shoes. Was our home a hotbed of toxic chemicals? Was I already ruining his life? How could I be trusted with this little life? The sense of responsibility was enormous and every decision felt fraught and momentous.

As a new mother, I was constantly measuring my mothering against some mysterious standard and finding myself flawed. Daniel didn't worry this way. I worried enough for both of us. I was wrapped up in my identity not only as a parent, but as the parent that got it right. I tried to avoid obsessing, but the voices out there telling mothers what they should and shouldn't be doing were compelling and perplexing. If I didn't worry about Zev, I felt that I wasn't being a good mother.

The first few months had been clean and simple, but as he grew, Zev's needs became more complex and his care required more decision-making and energy. At the same time, I seemed to be losing energy. I couldn't do the necessary chores. Dishes were left unwashed. Dirty laundry piles grew. We ate more frozen pizza.

I grasped to control whatever I could because the reality of having a real-live baby woke me up to how much extra work it is to get everything right and righteous. I was tired most of the time, bone tired, and couldn't imagine doing all of the things I had planned to do and thought I should be doing. I got stressed out at Daniel for not sharing my worries and not complying with my obsessions.

"You gave him what?!" I attacked Daniel one night.

"Well, I was eating some of that nice strawberry yogurt and I thought, 'I bet Zev would like this,' so I tried it. And, yup, he likes strawberry yogurt." Daniel had a big grin on his face. "You should have seen his little body wriggle to get more of it faster."

"Daniel! That yogurt has a ton of sugar in it. Remember we weren't going to give him any sugar for the first while? Oh, how could you have done that?"

"It was just a little yogurt."

"Oh, Daniel . . . ."

Such a reaction wasn't completely beyond the pale for an ambitious new mother hyped up on post-pregnancy hormones. The fatigue made the work twice as hard and wreaked havoc with my emotions. Thus, much of what I had intended to be as a parent simply flitted away, leaving me with only the residue of mother guilt and a grasping desire to believe I could still be the perfect mother if only I tried a little harder.

—

"SAM, YOU'VE BEEN complaining about this for a few weeks now. Go see the doctor and make sure it's nothing more serious. Then you can let it go," Daniel encouraged me while finishing the dishes from the night before. I sat nursing Zev, wincing when he accidentally punched the swollen node.

It's not that I was avoiding the doctor, but going to the doctor did not yet have a place in the intense routine of the baby zone I was in. I carried an undercurrent of uneasiness about what this swollen lymph node might represent. I did have a family history of cancer, but I rationalized that it was just a little lymph node and I was younger than most of the relatives who had had cancer. Eventually, however, the pain became loud enough that I had to call the doctor.

11

TO MY RELIEF, the doctor diagnosed a simple infected lymph node. When it disappeared with the prescribed antibiotic, I put it out of my head. I was still fatigued, but wasn't every new mother? And then, a few weeks later, multiple lymph nodes swelled up in my neck. I looked like a frog sometimes and made *ribbit* sounds to entertain Zev when I changed his diaper.

Back I went to my doctor, who diagnosed mono this time. I listened to him describe the symptoms of mono.

Swollen lymph nodes. Check.

Fatigue. Check. I fell asleep constantly.

Larger than normal liver. Check.

Check? I thought I had some leftover baby fat. My doctor had recommended sit-ups. Now I learned it was a fat liver.

The mono theory appeared to be a fit. I rolled the idea around in my head. Mono I could live with. It wasn't great, but it was manageable. There was no treatment for mono except to rest, look after myself and ride it out. This was not so easy with a nine-month-old and Daniel preparing to launch another busy and intense season of his artistic landscaping company. I had taken on some freelance work, so my days consisted of a steady cycle of work, baby food preparation, feeding, and cleaning up the food that Zev managed to spread on himself, me and the floor in his enthusiasm for his new skill of eating. Sisyphus had his rock and I had laundry. I didn't know how parents did it with multiple children.

As time passed, my motor slowed down even further. I fell asleep over my work at the computer. I fell asleep while nursing Zev. I dragged myself around to get things done. Daniel, seeing my exhaustion, gave me the gift of a massage for my birthday in May when Zev was about ten months old. I managed to eke out a day that was completely mine. Work and Zev were left under the care of others, housework was ignored.

The massage clinic was painted in soothing colours and there was no dirty laundry to be seen. I sank into the massage table to enjoy being kneaded and stroked by skilled hands. The massage therapist rubbed fragrant oils onto my tired bones and caressed my body into a relaxed state. I melted; I was without form. I floated through the evening and then sank into a relaxed, deep sleep.

Everything changed overnight.

"Daniel, wake up."

"What?" he mumbled.

"Wake up. There's something really wrong."

"Is it Zev?" Daniel said, popping upright.

"No, Daniel. Look at me. All sorts of lymph nodes have swollen up in the night. They're throbbing. Oh, Daniel, I don't think this is mono!" I said through tears.

I called my doctor and he told me to go directly to emergency at the hospital to meet with an internist. Up until that moment, I had been looking at this situation with my eyes half-closed, letting the lines blur and hoping that whatever was happening in my body would move along with time. But with this new development, I had to open my eyes and be a grown-up.

12

THE INTERNIST WALKED me through an extensive list of questions. She examined the nodes and she examined my belly. "Do you have any family history of cancer?" she asked, pushing her glasses back up her nose.

"Well, three of my grandparents died of cancer in their seventies. My father died of leukemia a few days before he turned sixty. My mother has been treated successfully for breast cancer."

She pursed her lips and frowned as she said, "We need more information. I'm scheduling you for a lymph node biopsy as soon as possible."

—

A WEEK LATER, I headed to the hospital for the biopsy. I checked in for the procedure and was handed a blue hospital gown with a curt, "Opens in back," and a finger point in the direction of a door. The change room was chilly as I pulled on the thin covering. Once in the appropriate attire, I was warehoused, alone, in a wheelchair, in the part of the hospital that had not yet been renovated. The paint that was once yellow had settled into mangy beige, with fine cracks running through it. The dotted linoleum on the floor was graying and edged in black. The ceiling tiles had faded to a greasy yellow. I felt like an abandoned piece of junked equipment. I was cold with my bare legs sticking out, white, skinny and goose-fleshed, from underneath the gown.

I was finally wheeled in and prepped for surgery. On the operating table, a green curtain kept me from seeing the bottom half of my body where they would be removing a lymph node from my groin area. It felt surreal to be lying down surrounded by a team clad in green scrubs and masks. I felt exposed and vulnerable.

For a biopsy like this they kept me awake, but the bottom half of my body felt like wet wool. Being awake, I was able to listen in on the operating room conversation.

"Did you see the game last night?" the surgeon asked the others. I couldn't hear their answers before he jumped in, "The Jays trounced the Tigers six to nothing. The Tigers didn't stand a chance." Shouldn't he have been paying attention to the surgery rather than baseball?

No one else in the room responded.

"Did you hear? Detroit is building a new stadium but it's keeping its location hidden from the public."

He waited a beat.

"Yeah, they're afraid the Tigers will find out where it is and try to play there."

The surgeon cackled at his own joke. One of the nurses made a polite laugh. The other nurse stayed quiet and the anesthesiologist grunted. And on it went through the operation.

Then the surgeon quietened, and I felt more pressure. I looked over and could see his shoulders straining with effort. He broke the silence with a long whistle.

"Whoa, did you ever see a baby like that?" he cried as he freed the lymph node from my resisting body and held it up for all to see. I turned away and shut my eyes. I was reminded of the joke: "What do they call the person who graduates at the bottom of the medical school class?"

"Doctor."

——

THEN CAME THE agonizing wait for a diagnosis. I was balanced on the razor-thin edge of a fence, waiting to see on which side I would land. It seemed as arbitrary as a coin toss. Heads, I would return to the land of a "normal" life; tails, I would fall off the fence into the land of SERIOUS ILLNESS, dragging my family down with me. Landing there would turn our beautiful little world upside down.

I tried to stay balanced on the fence while I waited, but the mind tends to chase the darkest possibilities. I walked around in a zombie-like state, barely able to look at Zev without crying, sure that I was a marked woman.

Friends and acquaintances didn't hesitate to share their theories and their stories.

"Oh, I had a cousin who..."

"Nothing to worry about, it's a treatable kind of cancer..."

"Well, my aunt Kit died of this kind of cancer..."

I dreaded cancer. It was probably cancer. My family history hovered over me like a vulture.

——

"I HAVE THE results back," are five of the most harrowing words in the English language. Individually benign, they are menacing in their synergy. When a doctor starts with, "I have the results back," you know it can't be good. Otherwise they would start with, "Good news!"

How many people have braced themselves against those words? How many people, like us, imagined a future unfolding with unswerving forward movement, only to have that movement halted in its tracks at the sound of those words? Perhaps, like going to war, those who have been through a moment like this understand something different about the world. There's no escaping a diagnosis, no escaping the reality of your body, no escaping the necessary redirection of your life. No matter who you are, no matter how you live, no matter how much money you have, no matter how many doctors you know, in reality, you are powerless against the force of those words.

"I have the results back," said the internist, perched on the edge of her desk right in front of me.

She looked down at her notes, her face settled into grim determination. The results of my lymph node biopsy were not supposed to be ready that day, so we had decided that Daniel would stay home with Zev while I came to what was supposed to be a quick checkup. But here we were with results and she was going to tell me my fate. I was alone, unprepared, feeling the emptiness of the chair beside me.

Everything became still except for the hum of the fluorescent lights, the ticking of her desk clock, muffled noises from the hallway. I sat upright, my hands clenched around the vinyl seat of my chair, my mouth pressed into a thin line, fairly certain that I was about to hear, "You have cancer."

Instead, she said, "You have something called amyloidosis."

As I registered her words, I let out my breath and said, "That's great!" with a big grin. No cancer. I had sidestepped my family's genetic legacy. I relaxed back in my chair and looked at the doctor, but she only looked concerned. My smile disappeared.

"Isn't it good that I don't have cancer?" I leaned forward again.

"No... not really. This is a bone marrow disease that's very serious... life-threatening. We need to get you to someone more specialized than me as quickly as possible."

I felt the fireball land in my stomach and begin to burn its way through my body, leaving me speechless. I didn't know what to do with this pronouncement. At the age of thirty-three, I was facing an unknown illness and the possibility of an early exit. I could not think.

13

I LEANED IN THE doorway and watched Daniel feed Zev with airplane motions and noises. Zev would giggle like a madman and then open his mouth ready to receive the squish-squash we had made. Not that he needed incentive to eat. Our boy was an eating machine. I had had to stop nursing him earlier than planned because of my fatigue and had cried and grieved, but Zev never looked back. Food was a way better deal—more flavour, more texture, less work.

The tableau of the two of them was almost too perfect. A little bomb was soon going to disturb the peace filling this room and I held off as long as I could. Daniel finally noticed me and said, "Hey, how was the appointment?" as he spooned another mouthful. He looked over at me then: "Sam, what's wrong?"

"She had the results. She gave me my diagnosis."

I came in and sat down beside Zev.

"I wasn't supposed to get the diagnosis today, but she had it and I had to get it all alone." I stroked Zev's head as he started kicking his feet up and whining in protest at the hold-up on the food. Daniel resumed feeding, but without the airplane noises or any sense of playfulness. He was waiting for the news. Zev didn't seem to care as long as the food kept coming.

"I've got something called amyloidosis."

"Ami... what?"

"Amyloidosis. It's a rare bone marrow disease... I have to go see a specialist as soon as possible... she said it's very serious... life-threatening. Oh, Daniel, this is big."

Daniel's face crumpled and he looked at me with intense, worried eyes.

I watched Zev eat. Whereas before my diagnosis I had seen him surrounded by sunshine, I now saw a threatening black pit around him, with mysterious dark creatures. What would a motherless life be like for him? I had to see him through his childhood. I had to help launch him into the world.

—

THE COMPUTER SCREEN glowed in the darkening room as I typed in a–m–y–l–o–i–d–o–s–i–s, checking the spelling against the crumpled piece of paper that lay on the desk. My internist had written out the name for me in her careful hand and I had absently stuffed the paper in my pocket. She had looked me in the eyes with a sad expression while she shook my hand and wished me the best. I don't remember answering her or remember how I got home.

I watched the hourglass on the screen, tapping my fingers until a list appeared. Near the top of the results was the Mayo Clinic website for *amyloidosis*. I clicked on the link and found my first definition:

> Amyloidosis is a disease that occurs when substances called amyloid proteins build up in your organs. Amyloid is an abnormal protein usually produced by cells in your bone marrow that can be deposited in any tissue or organ.

I read more definitions with terms like "abnormal cells," "abnormal proteins," "abnormal folding" and "abnormal depositions."

I found studies. I found a few self-help pages. But the more I read, the less I understood. I rubbed my eyes and tried to make sense of what I was reading and understand the implications for my future. The Cleveland Clinic website informed me that about ten people out of a million contracted the illness. I learned that most people with amyloidosis were closer to retirement age than child-bearing age. These odds made me feel as if I had won some sort of twisted lottery. Maybe a garden-variety cancer would have been better than this bizarre, unknown illness full of abnormalities. Something more conventional and mainstream might have made me feel less alone, less vulnerable, less like I was moving through uncharted ground. Of course, no one offered me the choice of which deadly disease I would like to be stricken with.

As I wandered through the web, I came across pictures of amyloid patients with horrible growths on their faces or with grotesque, misshapen tongues. I read obituaries and memorials for amyloid patients. I kept searching for amyloid survivor stories, flipping faster and faster through the pages, but I gave up after the twentieth page of search results.

It was getting dark, but I didn't bother to turn on the lights. Daniel came into the study and stood behind me looking at the screen, his hands on my shoulders. His fingers tightened as I sat motionless with the tears dripping down my face.

14

As soon as they heard about my diagnosis, my sisters and their spouses, all doctors, kicked into gear. They researched and talked to colleagues, circling in on the doctor in Toronto who had the most experience with this strange illness. They explained unfamiliar terms to me and talked about treatment options. They came with me to my early Toronto appointments, trying to hide their worry behind their professional demeanour.

I called them my A team—my Albert team. Both my sisters were beautiful and whip smart. My oldest sister, Shelley, was a nephrologist (kidneys). She was dark-haired, with a slightly exotic look that stood out from the pastiness of the rest of us. As the oldest sibling, she was steady and had almost stood outside of the fray when Lori and I fought as kids. One of my favourite memories is a camping trip in Nova Scotia when we were about fourteen, twelve and eight. Our parents were outside in a storm setting up tents while Shelley crouched in the front seat of the car and entertained Lori and me in the back with a stuffed lobster performing French cooking shows.

Lori, the middle daughter, grew up to be a rheumatologist (arthritis and other disorders of the joints, muscles and ligaments). She was fine-boned and blond and our faces, when we were young, were very similar. "Oh, you must be Lori Albert's little sister." Or, with a sigh, "Gee, your sister, Lori, was so much better than you at gym class." The resemblance has all but disappeared, but because Lori also teaches medical students, I meet many doctors who say, "Oh, you're Lori Albert's sister. Oh, I just love Lori!" We might have fought with verbal attacks when we were young, but that all disappeared as adults.

I am very lucky to have the sisters that I do. I love them ferociously. And they both chose kind, loving and interesting partners. Shelley's partner Cindy is a psychiatrist and Lori's husband Joel is an emergency physician.

In fact, if we stretched out beyond my immediate family to my extended family, it was pretty hard to swing a cat without hitting another doctor. Here was my running total:

1 nephrologist
1 rheumatologist
1 psychiatrist
1 emergency room doctor
1 oncologist
1 pediatric neurologist
2 cardiologists
1 internist
1 pediatrician
2 neurologists
1 gastroenterologist
1 radiologist

I was the baby of the family. The not-a-doctor. Someone had to be the patient.

—

FROM EARLY ON, my sisters had both known they wanted to pursue medicine. This may have been partly cultural. My parents strongly believed in having a profession and it was enlightened of them to encourage their three daughters to pursue what had been traditionally male careers. When my mother was growing up, you married a doctor. When we were growing up, you became a doctor.

My sisters, committing themselves to their training, disappeared into the abyss of medical school. I wouldn't see them for days on end as they stayed up all night on call or closed themselves up in their rooms to study. Even when exhausted, their eyes would light up to indicate their excitement for their subject matter if you asked the right question.

I watched my sisters with awe but had no desire to join them. I had never been able to bear seeing or hearing about other people's injuries. If I happened to find out about an accident or an injury, a cold dread would slime down my torso to my feet. It didn't even need to be serious; a stubbed toe could have as much impact as a gruesome cut. I knew that a doctor who could not stand the sight or even the sound of an injury was of no use.

But I was sometimes tempted by the yearly medical school variety show. Those medical students (my sisters included) could sing, play instruments, act, and dance with as much talent as they could take a case history or stitch a cut. I would sit in the audience with my parents, longing to be up on the stage, knowing I could make an excellent contribution to this medical school institution. Entering medicine so I could star in the medical school variety show was not the same as having a calling, though, so I would be the "not-a-doctor" of the family.

"You're lucky. I could be into drugs or prostitution; instead, I'm going to *theatre school!*" I would remind my parents.

"Okay," said my mother. "I think you would be a great doctor, but if that's not the career you want, there is always law school."

When I was younger, I hadn't appreciated all of the doctors in the family. I had even found it annoying sometimes when everyone assumed I would follow suit. I admired my sisters but being surrounded by so many doctors left me feeling that it was almost too easy to pursue medicine. It was simply the thing everyone did and, yawn, I would do something more interesting. But there I was, facing a monster illness and grateful to the tips of my toes that I had such skilled sister–doctors in my court. And, really, with my gained knowledge combined with the amount of time spent in hospitals and clinics over the years, you could say that I did go into medicine after all. Being the youngest, however, I had to go into it *my* way.

—

WE FOUND OUR way to the best doctor for this weird disease, a hematologist at Princess Margaret Hospital in Toronto who specialized in rare bone marrow disorders and who saw more amyloid patients than anyone else in Canada, maybe twenty a year. He wasted no time in arranging for me to be what they called "staged." I spent days at the hospital being poked, scanned, covered in goop and made to hold my breath. I had to collect my pee in a jug for twenty-four hours and my hematologist performed the painful bone marrow test, popping out a core sample of my bone marrow for examination as if I were a tree. A second lymph node was removed and examined for the presence of amyloid.

There was no sneaking away from this world as I had done when my father was ill; I had to claim it as my own.

—

MY SISTER SHELLEY and I sat with one of the many doctors consulted in the diagnostic process. He was trying to help me understand this strange illness.

"With amyloidosis, the bone marrow produces too much of the amyloid protein, a protein we all have. The excess protein accumulates in different parts of the body, depending on the person. You have excess protein in your liver, spleen and lymph nodes."

My look must have been vacuous because he switched tactics.

"Imagine a car factory humming along smoothly. Each machine makes a different part of the car."

I pictured a factory in my body: the hum of assembly lines, workers in jumpsuits armed with protective goggles and ear protection, lots of robotic arms shuffling parts.

"Now imagine someone leaves the fender-making machine on all night."

I pictured a quiet factory with one little machine left on autopilot. Shiny fenders were being dropped off from this one machine onto a series of conveyor belts that transported these surplus fenders to the different car assembly lines, one of which was my liver.

"Ah," I said in sudden comprehension. "My problem is that I have too many fenders! And they are genuinely fond of my liver." I pictured my liver as a magnet with thousands of little fenders on it.

But I realized I still didn't completely understand. The amyloid proteins were not themselves toxic. What harm could they do?

"The amyloid is sticky, like beeswax, and builds up. It can start to affect the way an organ functions." I imagined a healthy organ trying to operate normally while encased in thick, heavy beeswax. I saw in my mind a picture of my heart or kidneys being slowly strangulated by these relentless amyloid proteins, or my vessels being clogged up with amyloid the way a milkshake might clog up a straw, interfering with circulation. I began to understand the gravity of the situation.

Shelley squeezed my hand.

PART FOUR

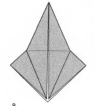

8.

9.

15

THE STANDARD FIRST-LINE treatment for amyloidosis is a stem-cell transplant, also known as a stem-cell rescue. Stem cells are like first-year undergraduate students in a general arts or science degree. At first, they are a group of fuzzy, unformed blobs in their massive first-year classes. Whether it's PSYCH 101 or Introduction to English Literature, they blend together, seemingly interchangeable in their texting/Instagram-obsessing/insecure/wet-behind-the-ears ways. As they get older and move into graduate school, they start to differentiate themselves into specialty subjects such as Hydrology Engineering and Evolutionary Linguistics.

Stem cells, likewise, start off as undifferentiated cells. That is, they are like the undecided undergraduates. They then develop into specialized cells to meet the body's needs. In my case, my stem cells now needed to do a graduate degree in bone marrow with subspecialties in red blood cells, white blood cells and platelets.

In other words, this treatment would deliver a huge whack of chemo to destroy cells in my bone marrow that, instead of pursuing higher education, had gotten mixed up with booze and drugs and were insidiously producing amyloid. But the chemo wasn't particularly smart; it would wipe out the whole bone marrow, not just the abnormal cells.

After the chemo had done its job, the stem cells that would have been harvested from me before the transplant would come rushing in, fresh-faced, to save the day. These stem cells would rebuild the bone marrow and, hopefully, not go off the rails as some of their predecessors had.

This treatment scared the shit out of me. I would be given a potentially deadly dose of chemo and then left without an immune system for a number of days. There was always the possibility that my stem cells wouldn't rebuild my bone marrow or that I would reject them when they were reinfused. I would feel like crap and experience any number of side effects. I wouldn't be able to have much contact with Zev throughout the roughly two weeks I would be in hospital because of my vulnerability to infection. And I could go through the whole thing and still be as sick as I was when I started.

Underlying it all was the deep fear of leaving my family with an aching hole. Visions of Zev crying for me and of Daniel trying to comfort him without success often invaded my thoughts and made me weak. My fears were always with me and they were loud. As if I were trapped in a car with pounding heavy metal music, the beat penetrating my body and providing the background noise to every single thing I did.

I had to prepare myself, I had to do something to help control this worrying. I had to feel as if I had some agency in this situation. The transplant was scheduled for November. I had four months to prepare.

—

"DANIEL?" I HOVERED in the doorway of the study, watching him sort through piles of papers.

"Yes, love."

"Marsha called from the Tai Chi Centre. There's a big program going on there, an instructor training. There are going to be people from all over the world and many of the senior instructors who worked with Master Moy. She said it would make a lot of sense for me to go up and ask for their advice and help when they are all together. They've agreed to me coming and Marsha has made a bed available in her room. So, if I wanted, it would work for me to go. What do you think?"

"I think you should go." Daniel didn't hesitate.

"Really?! What about Zev?"

"It will be fine. I'm caught up right now. Yeah, go."

—

THE FIRST TIME I put my back out I was eighteen, feet sticking out of the bathroom door as I lay, unable to move, waiting for my parents' return. Over the years, I had spent hours—days—in bed from lifting something the wrong way, wearing the wrong shoes, slouching. I had a bad, bad back.

When I was twenty-five, I met a long-time instructor with the Taoist Tai Chi Society who told me that tai chi could help my back. She was right. Over the ensuing years, I became able to control my back problems through the tai chi practice. I was able to relax muscles that had been tight for as long as I could remember. I improved my alignment, worked on my balance, opened up cramped spaces.

I also learned that I had joined something that was far more than an exercise club. This charitable organization was a community and a place to develop as a person, as well as to help other people achieve better health.

By the time I was diagnosed in 2000, I had become a volunteer instructor and volunteer treasurer for our local branch. I had been to retreats and had met Master Moy Lin Shin, the Taoist monk who had come from Hong Kong to share the Taoist arts and had founded this charitable organization. Until his death in 1998, Master Moy dedicated his life to helping people. He was our Teacher with a capital T.

The International Taoist Tai Chi Centre north of Toronto offered monthly workshops for people struggling with health problems that made it difficult for them to attend a regular retreat. I remember two trains of thought running through my mind when I heard of this. One voice said, "Oh, isn't this great for *those* people, those sick people, to have a place like this," as if sick people were a separate species. At the same time, I remember thinking, "If anything big befalls my family or me, I know this is where I'll come."

—

THE INTERNATIONAL CENTRE was situated on a hundred acres of land at the edge of the Hockley Valley north of Toronto. Master Moy had had the vision in the early days of the organization to have the Society purchase a centre where people could stay, a place that would focus the training and revitalize individuals to go back out and help people in their local communities. When I arrived for my week in 2000, I was joining hundreds of other participants from across Canada and around the world.

I went to as many of the sessions as I could and slept a great deal. I met with some of the more senior instructors and directors, those who had trained for many years and who had a deep understanding of the Taoist arts. I laid out my story for them. They were supportive and suggested that I increase the level of my practice in order to better handle the upcoming treatment. They told me that I would want to be as strong as possible and it would be worth investing the time before I went into hospital. They invited me to come to Toronto and spend time in one of our locations in Chinatown working with a senior instructor there. They said, "Come and work hard." So, I did.

———

THAT TIME, THOSE four months between diagnosis and treatment—the limbo between knowledge and action—is a period of time that weighs heavily in our family narrative. Daniel was a mess, with his own set of worries, although at the time, it was hard for me to perceive it, being so wrapped up in my own mess. He was worried about losing me, of course. On top of that, he was also supporting the family financially with his artistic landscaping company. He was in the third season of his business and the work was intense, overwhelming and time sensitive. Because his business was still small, he had to do designs and the associated quotes, meet with clients, go on plant runs, do the bookkeeping, work outside with his crew and perform any other administrative tasks that had to be done. He could not yet afford to hire the help he needed. He worried about angry clients. He worried about the mistakes his staff might make. He worried about making enough money to support us.

Intellectually I could see what was happening, I could see how much stress he was under. But the level of fatigue I was facing, combined with the volume of my fears, crowded out my ability to truly take notice of his struggles. Besides, my situation was life and death. In my mind, this outranked any other problems. I felt certain that devoting myself to tai chi was vitally important for my health, and therefore our family, even though it meant that I was often away and would leave Daniel with an outsized burden of care. I just didn't know what else to do.

I've stewed for years about the choice I made and whether or not it was the right one. Some cheered me on, others commented to me or to Daniel that they thought I should be home with my family. My compromise was to go but feel guilty about it. When I'm thinking clearly, I realize that I had no real choice at all. It was all I could do at the time. And it wasn't easy.

—

TWIST STEP, STAND up, turn the body, place the foot, let the hands go, shift the weight.

Repeat on the other side.

On and on, for hours.

Twist step, stand up, turn the body, place the foot, let the hands go, shift the weight.

Repeat on other side.

That was the rhythm of my days leading up to my stem-cell transplant. I was doing "brush knees," a move from the tai chi set that is helpful to practice in long rows, back and forth. My instructor would sometimes guide me with a new correction. "Let the hand go faster." "Drop the weight more."

Other times he would tell me to forget everything and keep moving... to relax... to let it go. *Fung son* is a word in Cantonese that means, roughly, looseness and letting go. Letting go is what I was struggling to do. Letting go of my constant anxiety. Letting go of the fears that clung to me like cockleburs. Letting go of anything that was not important at that moment.

As I moved through the room, I experienced moments when everything felt lovely and open in my body, as if my big liver had disappeared; as if I was hollow, filled with lightness. There were moments when I was, indeed, able to "let it all go." Moments when I could feel the weight concentrate down into my feet. I felt as relaxed as a Gumby doll, practically drunk with the release. My colour improved. My appetite was restored. I felt stronger. I could do the tai chi for longer without stopping.

In fact, there were times when I felt so well that I wondered if the disease had gone into a spontaneous remission. This thought was reinforced by the perception that my liver was shrinking. Every day I would lie on the floor and Mary, one of my tai chi friends, would outline what appeared to be the reducing liver size on my stomach with a felt-tip pen. I'd feel the tickle of the pen and see the expression of excitement on Mary's face as she felt for the edges of the liver. Her smile would widen as she saw the marked area shrink. I perceived the change on the inside as well. It felt as if I had more room to breathe, room to move, room to eat.

I took the telltale pen marks and my feeling of wellness back to my doctor, requesting another bone marrow test to be absolutely sure I was still sick. It seems ridiculous now— magical thinking—but at the time, I could not reconcile how well I felt with the reality of my diagnosis. My doctor humoured me and repeated this test, which is both painful and, I'm sure, expensive, with no change in the results. I still carried the disease, but I didn't feel as sick as I had. Maybe I could be a really healthy sick person.

I kept up the intense practice. Often, I had to force myself to do "one more row." And then another. And then another. I wanted to kick back and relax. I wanted to do something that wasn't tai chi. I wanted to be home with my family. But

I kept going. I had a panicky feeling that if I didn't do enough tai chi, I wouldn't make it. No one had suggested this to me, but deep down I believed it. It was the only control I had in this situation.

As the practice progressed over the weeks, I felt happier and stronger, like I owned my body again; it did not belong to the disease. I would feel like the world was a beautiful place and I could handle anything coming my way. I would feel joy. And I would know, deeply, in my body, that this was what I needed to get through this next phase of my life.

And then I would call Daniel and Zev in the evening and I would deflate. I would gurgle at Zev and listen to his coos through tears. When did he learn how to make those new sounds? How could he be growing and changing without me? Could I be a good mother if I wasn't even there? As I started feeling better, it was easy to forget what I had felt like before. And it was harder for Daniel to understand why I still needed to be away so much. How could I tell him how joyful I felt when he was so burdened and miserable?

On the phone, Daniel would ask, "When are you coming home, Sam?" Sometimes the question came out as a wistful love that gently wrapped around my heart. Other times, the stress in his voice clenched my stomach tight with guilt. This question was the bellwether of Daniel's state of mind. All I could do was whisper, "Soon."

—

"DANIEL, I'M HEADING out to the tai chi club to practice."

He appeared at the top of the stairs holding Zev, who couldn't get enough of playing with Daniel's impressive nose.

"Sam, you're only home for a few days and you're going out to practice?" I could see the bags under his eyes and the slope of his shoulders.

"My instructors said I need to be practicing all the time."

"Your instructors don't come here and look after our son. Zev needs you. I need you," Daniel replied in a sharp tone.

Logic and love were telling me to stay home and give Daniel a break. My panic and fear were loud, however.

"Daniel, the transplant is so soon, and I need to be ready. I'm so scared." I turned and opened the door. "I'm so sorry, I'll take over Zev as soon as I get back." Then I was gone.

My end of the bargain for survival was to work as hard as I could. And survival superseded everything else. I recalled my worry about being too selfish to have children. Was that selfishness manifesting itself now? With my illness thrown into the mix, I was constantly weighing my actions to see if they were selfish or self-care. Sometimes Daniel told me stories of how his mother had always been there for her kids. He didn't mean it as a direct jab, but in a reminiscence of joy. That was what a mother was, from his experience.

The chatter inside my own head didn't help: *How could you leave your baby? A mother's place is with her baby. You are a bad mother for leaving your child so much.* So, I'd try to stay home more. But it was a Catch-22. When I was home and doing less tai chi, I was weaker. I spent more time in bed and more time crying. My mind would circle in on itself and go to the darkest places; courage would fail. I was home in body, but I couldn't be of much help or be very present. On the other hand, when I was in Toronto and focused on the tai chi and working on my health, I felt transformed. I had more energy, I felt brave, I did not feel the burden of my large liver, I felt alive. But I was leaving Daniel alone to work gruelling and stressful days running an emerging business and caring for Zev. I left Daniel to fend for himself emotionally and closed myself off to him.

I had to keep reminding myself why I was making those choices, why I needed to be away. Otherwise I might have gone running home to smell Zev's sweet baby head. An insightful friend pointed out more than once that working hard to have a future was the best thing I could do for Zev. Nevertheless, I was tormented by my decision.

While I was grateful for how the tai chi gave me physical and emotional strength to handle the stem-cell transplant, I never stopped feeling like the cost of my choice for the family had been high and that I was at fault for the extra stress in our lives.

16

GROWING UP, I believed that girls with long hair had a better life than mine. I can still remember my face turning hot as I walked into my kindergarten class the first day, hearing whispers of "She looks like a boy." My mother liked my hair short and, with the exception of the year I acted as one of Jesus's long-haired apostles in *Jesus Christ Superstar* in Grade Ten, my hair was always on the short side. In public school I envied the pigtails and braids of other girls. As I grew older, I believed that if I had long hair, I would be more beautiful, more popular, and my quality of life would have to improve.

Thus, the minute I left home, I started growing my hair until I had a thick, long mane. I learned to make buns and chignons and other concoctions with my beautiful locks, and I used metal rods to make my braids stick out like Pippi Longstocking on Halloween. I sported long, dangly earrings to go with the hair and cultivated a hippy, granola look. I was vain about my hair, luxuriating in its thick texture and natural colour (the same colour as girl-detective Nancy Drew; Titian blonde, which I pronounced *tit-ee-an* blonde for years). Finally, I had achieved the look I had yearned for. My husband loved my long hair and I loved him loving it. Yes, I did believe my life was better with long hair.

Then came the day when I was introduced to the chemotherapy that was associated with my stem-cell transplant.
The doctor ran through the side effects I could expect:
mouth sores, diarrhea, hair loss ... While he continued
down the list my brain stopped at hair loss. As much as I
thought of myself as strong and practical, my vanity knocked
on the door. My thick, beautiful hair, of which I was so proud,
would disappear, eaten up by the strong medication. I was
floored by this thought almost as much as the news of the
diagnosis itself. I cried for several days, contemplating life
bald, wondering if Daniel would still think I was beautiful,
wondering how Zev would react to a bald mother. What if
the hair didn't grow back?

But I started to bore myself with my tears. I was very
good at intense wallowing, but not long-term wallowing. I
had a desire to take action, to be proactive in dealing with
the anguish I was feeling about this loss. I decided to cut my
hair off before the treatment and get the grieving over with.
I felt strong and mature making this decision.

I made an appointment with my hairdresser and left Daniel and Zev to await my new appearance. My hands were
tight on the steering wheel as I turned into the parking lot.
I sat in the car a moment, trying to decide if this was a good
idea or not. Then I sighed and made my way into the salon.

Lori Ann, the brash hairdresser with whom I entrusted
my hair, was finishing the blow dry on a woman with long,
silky black hair. I yearned after this hair as I watched Lori
Ann run the dryer and the brush over it again and again in
long smooth strokes. This woman would take her hair home
with her.

Lori Ann came to sit beside me on the couch to see what
kind of a cut I wanted. She had dyed blonde hair and wore

heavy mascara. I liked her; she was tough. I looked at the floor and spurted out, "Lori Ann, I'm going to have chemo and lose my hair. I want a short haircut now. I don't want to be weeping over my hair when I'm getting chemo." I managed to get this out in a rush without crying.

Lori Ann sat and listened to the whole story, making exclamations at all the right moments. She led me to the chair, patted my arm and went to work.

"Sam, you have nothing to worry about. I've had a ton of clients who've lost their hair and it always grows back. You wear one of those kerchief thingies. I think you should get one in green; it will look really good. Or maybe you could get a wig. That's it. Get a wig in some outrageous colour. I knew of a woman who did that and then met her husband out at a restaurant, and he said it was like having an affair while still being with his wife." Lori Ann talked on and the words were soothing.

As she cut, I watched my long auburn locks drift onto the wooden floor and bit my lip. My neck was suddenly exposed. My forehead felt naked. I didn't recognize the person in the mirror. What had I done?

"There. Take a look. I think you look fantastic."

Unfortunately, Lori Ann had given me something more like a mullet than I had intended which, in and of itself, was quite traumatic. I tried not to cry while I was still in her shop, but my twisted-up face gave me away. She gave me a hug as I was leaving. "It will grow again, honey."

I hoped she was right.

I was anxious about how fourteen-month-old Zev would react to this major change in my looks. Would he cry in terror at this stranger approaching to pick him up? Would it take him weeks to get used to me?

When I arrived home, Daniel was at a loss for words. He was trying to be kind. For him, I don't think it was the short-ness that was the problem, but the mullet-ness of the haircut. He kept saying things like,

"Well, if you cut it like this it will look a whole lot better," or

"It looks like Tina Turner," said with a shudder.

This was not a good start. I promised to get it trimmed into a proper brush cut and he assured me it would look fine. "Fine" was not exactly what I was after, but maybe it was all I could expect at the moment.

Zev was waking up from a nap and I dragged myself up the stairs to his room. I walked in and waited for the screams and the tears.

Silence. Gurgle. Smile. Gurgle some more. No different from any other time. I had fretted all day about how he might react, and he didn't even notice a change. He reached his arms out to be picked up, his eyes looking into mine. I held him close and breathed in his scent deeply. He would always know me.

I eventually stopped experiencing a jolt of shock every time I spotted myself in a mirror. I found a barbershop that would trim my hair nicely into a brush cut and discovered that I had more time in the mornings now that I didn't need to fuss over hair. I didn't love how I looked, but overall, I felt that I had "let go" of my hair. I congratulated myself on handling the whole situation with great aplomb. Bring on the chemo.

17

I MET DEATH WHILE taking the Avenue Road bus to the hospital to begin my stem-cell transplant. It was October 31, although Halloween was not anywhere on my radar. Daniel was taking Zev to my mother's apartment and would meet me later. Sitting there on the faded red velveteen seat, not really seeing Avenue Road as it hurtled by, I brooded over my prospects. I was terrified of dying and my worked-up imagination projected forward to my funeral. My mind populated the sad event with my friends and family, crying and laughing and telling stories. I tried not to weep at the thought of the way they would circle around the grief of Daniel and Zev. And then I thought of my two boys, home alone after the funeral, and my body ached.

It had been my choice to take the bus by myself. I felt that I could be braver if I was alone. Just me and my backpack, striding into the hospital. There would be no one attempting to crack the shield I had built around myself, asking me if I was okay, asking me what I was feeling. However, as I stewed in my anxiety and obsessed about what was almost certainly my imminent death either from the treatment or from the disease, I wondered if I had made a mistake. Perhaps coming with Daniel by my side would have been a good idea. By myself, I wasn't so sure I would be striding in, after all.

I looked around the bus and saw two young boys in matching Spiderman costumes sitting at the back with their father.

"Smarties are way better than Oh Henrys!" the one yelled at the other. The father quieted them before I could hear the defense for the Oh Henry! chocolate bar. I wanted to live long enough to see Zev argue about Halloween candy. That thought set off my tears again.

The bus wheezed as it braked to a stop. More passengers mounted the stairs and paid their fares, putting wallets back into purses and pockets. Then there was a hush on the bus as the last figure rose up the stairs and paid a fare. Death looked around at the small group of travellers already seated and headed toward the back. His long black robe made a "swishswash" polyester sound as he approached. He lowered his scythe to avoid damaging the ceiling, which set him off balance as the bus started up again. He quickly righted himself, trying to maintain his dignified stance.

The death mask was skeletal with blank eye sockets, a wide-open mouth. His breathing through the mask sounded like Darth Vader. He settled himself into one of the seats, the people near him leaning away from his large presence. Sitting tall, Death turned his head with a majestic slowness to examine his surrounding kingdom. The two little boys had their mouths open with identical expressions of awe.

Had my absorption with my own demise somehow summoned the spectre of death on a downtown bus? I could not stop grinning. Of course, this might not appear to be a sane way to react to the presence of Death, but it was funny to me. Perhaps he would want to come to the hospital with me to get acquainted with the other patients. "No, no, he's with me!" I imagined reassuring them as we did the rounds. We could take our mocha lattes into the sunny atrium and watch the crowd, helping people normalize their own deaths with his regular presence. Maybe a lecture series, a speaker's tour. We could really go big, revealing the true secrets of death. I wondered if he would be up on the latest in the afterlife, or if he was strictly involved in the specifics of dying.

This representative of Death in front of me, jeans and sneakers peeking out from under his Halloween costume, was the jolt I needed to become unstuck. The more I spun these stories out about him, the less mired I felt in the bleakness of what I was about to face. I rang the bell for the next stop without hesitation and walked tall as I made my way to the doors and descended the steps, the heroine of my own movie. "She who survived a brush with death!" I chuckled to myself. I imagined the background music to be victorious as the camera followed my confident steps along the sidewalk and into the hospital.

18

A HICKMAN LINE IS inserted directly into your heart. Well, almost to your heart. It goes into a large vein near the heart. My first stop before being admitted was to have a Hickman line installed as a way of both delivering medication and drawing blood during my transplant. The surgeon was to make the incision in my chest, snake in some tubing and ensure that the tube was properly inserted into the vein. I was told it would be a minor procedure.

The surgeon assigned to me was young, and I wondered if he was still in training, because things did not go well. He tugged and fiddled with something that was connected to my heart, the very centre of my being. Over and over again, he tried to get it and missed and there was more fiddling and tugging and cursing. It felt as if an animal were loose in my body, gnawing away at my vessels, piercing me to my very essence.

I thought about my heart working away, miraculously, without complaint, day in and day out, protected by my ribs and soft tissue. But under the hand of this doctor, my heart felt vulnerable and exposed. I was in pain and deeply shaken. And the doctor continued to tug and fiddle and no one stepped in to help him. It hurt so much, and I wanted him to stop. I didn't know then that I could advocate for myself.

Finally he finished and he and the other doctors left. I lay there, trying to collect myself. The nurse came and sat me up, pointed to my clothes and told me I was done. I must have looked ghastly, but there was no hand holding or reassurances. I sat there a moment while they cleaned up and left. I moved very slowly, afraid that I might throw up.

Changing clothes wasn't easy with my fragile new wound. I was drained by the time I had settled the last layer of shirt and put my coat on. I looked at my backpack that I had so jauntily swung over my shoulders that morning. It had now become impossibly heavy. I stepped out into the empty hallway. There was no one there to ask for help; only miles of hallway.

After resting, I picked up the pack and began walking. The procedure had taken place at Toronto General Hospital, but I needed to get across University Avenue, a major arterial road, to Princess Margaret Hospital to be admitted for the transplant. I had crossed that road without thinking that morning. Now, in my hazy and fragile state, it looked as if University Avenue had grown while I'd been inside having my heart bruised. It had become a vast plain that I had to cross with speed. I wasn't doing speed. Every effort returned a little bit of pain and made me feel as if I might break.

The light changed in my favour and I shambled as quickly as I could, but I barely made it to the median before the light changed again. I waited there through two changes of the light, catching my breath and preparing myself for the next half. It continued on like this. Each leg of the journey was sandwiched by rest stops as well as a girding of the loins to keep moving toward this frightening treatment. If the procedure to put in the Hickman line was supposed to be the easy part, I was in trouble. What could I expect from the transplant itself?

I finally made it to the elevator. I was in pain and shaking with agitation and fear. I leaned against a wall for a few minutes to compose myself. Then I stepped forward and pushed the button for the fourteenth floor, although every molecule of my being wanted to turn and run.

At the nurse's desk they told me to wait in my assigned room and a nurse would come by soon to get me set up. I found my bed and dropped down onto it. Daniel was not there yet. He was supposed to have been there by the time I arrived.

I called my mother's house, my voice a high thin wire, "Where's Daniel?"

My mother's distress-o-meter was turned on, "What's wrong?"

"I need Daniel." I was trying to keep the tears out of my voice.

"He dropped Zev off and then left. He should be there soon. Can I do anything?"

"I just need Daniel; I'll call you later." Just the thing a worried mother wants to be told.

A nurse came in as I sat distraught and weepy.

"Now, now, let's have none of that," she chided. I stared at her, open-mouthed, a small pulse of rage forming underneath my distress as she plumped some pillows and then left again.

My sister in-law, Cindy, happened to stop by at that moment.

"Hi Sam, I wanted to see how you were settling in..." She stopped when she saw me up close. My appearance was startling. Not only was I white and weeping, but the red antiseptic the surgeon had basted on my chest made me look like I had a major burn. Because I couldn't stop crying, I couldn't convey to her that I was not crying because of what appeared to be a burn, but because I felt like someone had tugged my heart out and I felt lonely and afraid. All I could get out was that I needed to see Daniel. She understood and left, not wanting to impose.

Daniel finally walked in and I clung to him and cried and cried. After being so strong for so long, after containing myself so doggedly for months and months, the events of the day had pulled the stopper and all of the emotions were finally rushing out. It was as if my heart was truly pierced, creating a crack in the structure I had been so careful to maintain. The fear, worry, guilt, and anger overwhelmed me. I couldn't hold on anymore and all I could do was heave and cry and hold on to Daniel. Thank goodness he was there to catch me.

19

MY EVENING WITH Daniel helped me to ease and settle. The pain from the procedure was almost gone. I was calm and ready, holding Daniel's hand, when the team arrived to begin the transplant the next morning.

The first step was to give me a massive dose of a chemo drug called melphalan. They hooked me up and I watched every drop of the clear liquid drip into my body. I had imagined that it would be fluorescent green or bright orange, something that would indicate *danger* or *take notice*. I tried to decide whether I should look upon this drug as magic potion or poison. I couldn't believe I was choosing to have my entire immune system wiped clean. Was this rational?

I imagined the melphalan coursing through my body, eating up the bone marrow like Pac-Man, wiping me clean of cells. I was attentive to every nuance of how the drug made me feel. My scalp tingled. Were my hair follicles releasing their grip? Did I feel my eyebrows thinning? Was I feeling nauseous? Could I feel the mouth sores forming? Daniel and I both stared with wide eyes as this drug made its way into my body.

That's how I remember it happening, anyway. Daniel tells me that I fell asleep almost immediately because of the pre-meds they had given me to prevent nausea. So much for the power of memory.

From Roberta Albert
Sent: Thursday, November 9, 2000
Subject: Update for Wednesday, November 8

Hi Everyone,

It is Wednesday, November 8 and I am taking advantage of a few moments of quiet, while Zev is sleeping, to provide the latest report. It is a warm, but grey day in Toronto. The leaves are nearly all gone, but outside my window there is still a spotty, but glorious panorama of gold and orange.

Sam is now in an isolation room where she was moved Sunday night. This is the official "Day 2" of Sam's treatment. The counting began on Monday, Nov. 6th when her stem cells were restored to her, all 5 million of them. Monday was "Day 0". The expectation is that by Day 3, tomorrow, Sam will be feeling quite ill and, as her counts go down over the next four or five days, she will bottom. Then, as her stem cells begin to kick in, she will gradually start to feel better. Once her counts are high enough, she can come out of isolation. The average time in isolation is 12 days, assuming there are no complications, that puts us at a week Saturday. There is a large calendar in Sam's room and each day is struck off with a vengeance.

I need to close for now. My timing was perfect, because I now hear Zev crying. We are taking him to the hospital to see Sam. Daniel will meet us there to take him home for dinner. Shelley is babysitting tonight, so Dan can be at the hospital. Best of all, Dan's mother, Barbara Shoag is arriving on Monday to provide her personal support. It will be wonderful having her here. Happily, Dan's father, Leon, will join Barbara here next weekend.

Roberta

I sat in the window well of my hospital room, my prison, my nose pressed against the glass, trying not to feel sorry for myself. People were rushing to work or school. Did they know how free they were? A week earlier I had taken for granted the luxury of picking up my backpack and stepping out into sunshine or rain to go where I pleased.

I wasn't exactly locked in my room, but I was tethered to an IV machine and the chemo had flattened me to the degree that the best I could do was slither from bed to bathroom to window.

As I sat in my pajamas, almost bald, listless and too thin, it was hard not to feel that the whole world was rushing by and I was being left behind.

—

THE TRANSPLANT GAVE Daniel and me a brief reprieve from the pressure that had been testing our relationship. I was trapped in a room, and he agreed to be trapped with me for as many hours a day as he could sit still. Zev was bundled around to various family members. Daniel and I played cards, read the paper, listened to the radio. He would bring me treats and tell me stories of his adventures tootling around Toronto on a downhill ski converted into a skateboard that a friend had lent him. As I started to wilt and suffer from the treatment, he would fetch me Popsicles to ease my mouth sores or encourage me to get up and walk around the ward or do some tai chi.

We found each other again after the stress and separation of the previous months. It was a sweet time for us, which is a funny thing to say about such a huge and scary medical procedure. But the stem-cell transplant forced us to pause and

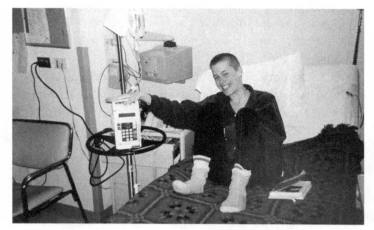

In hospital before the stem-cell transplant, feeling hopeful about the future

quiet our life. There was nothing to do but wait and fill the hours. This time helped us refuel emotionally for the life we would have to face again once I was released from hospital.

The transplant also gave me moments of quiet aloneness. I had no TV and it was a time before one could turn on the computer and power up a movie or game. The only phone I had was the hospital land line. Now I could breathe and think.

One night I was feeling lonely and rudderless and I remembered all of the journals I had been given before coming into hospital. I guess my friends had decided that I should journal this incredibly scary time. They were beautiful gifts, but I'd never really found journalling to be my thing.

I drew one out now. A small spiral-bound black one with a stylized moon and solar system on it. I didn't want to journal. I wanted to write. I had always been an academic writer, but creative writing had scared me. Now I wanted to write a children's story about what I was going through.

In preparation for my time in hospital, Daniel's mother Barbara had bought me the first two Harry Potter books. They had been a fun read, but I had also felt a kinship with Harry. He had had this particular quest thrust upon him; he had not gone chasing it. That's how I felt. This disease had been thrust upon me and it was like a quest I had to complete. I had to rise to it whether I liked it or not. When I thought that way, I wallowed and worried less, feeling instead like the brave hero of my own life. I had an idea for a story for young children about a lazy pig who liked to wallow in the mud who would be called upon to complete a quest that had come for him.

The story wasn't really any good, but after finishing it, I wanted to write more stories. And so, in the quiet of the hospital nights, I began to write. I discovered that I had things to say and liked trying to figure out how to say them. Later I wrote some poetry and short stories. Then I started to write my story.

We never choose these hard things, but if we're lucky, we'll stumble upon a spark that makes the misery bearable.

—

ALTHOUGH I WAS alone much of the time, a state I didn't mind when I was feeling low, there was much evidence of my relationships scattered about the room. Daniel's brother Michael and his wife Elisabeth had sent me a care package that included my new favourite rubber ducky pajamas. My tai chi friends had made a mobile of one thousand paper cranes, which, traditionally, is meant to bring good luck and good health. Additionally, Barbara organized paper crane making among her family members. I received dozens of colourful cranes from different cities. These cranes were an explosion of love. I was never truly alone.

—

I HAD BECOME used to the brush cut and thought I had been tough and mature about the whole hair thing. But as more hair accumulated on my pillow or came out as I ran my hand over my head, I looked patchy. I looked in the mirror despite myself and what I saw was discouraging. It was hard enough to feel sick without also looking like a trauma victim.

"Daniel," I shouted back into the room. "It's time to shave me."

Daniel came into the bathroom and stood beside me facing the mirror. His smile was far too eager and excited for how I was feeling.

"This is not a happy time, Daniel; this is really hard for me. Dial it back." He tried but couldn't completely close down his smile.

You could count on Daniel to get excited and enjoy the things that were difficult, nay, potentially traumatic, to other people. There had been a house fire at the farmhouse where we had been living with Susanna and friends when we first moved to Stratford. This house had belonged to Susanna's grandparents, with furniture she had inherited from them and precious pictures of them and other ancestors. While Susanna was in an understandable state of distress, Daniel bounced around like a little kid to see the fire trucks and the commotion. When a train we were on hit a truck, he was delighted with the whole accident scene, pushing his way to a better view, his excitement not at all dampened by the tragic state of the truck driver. He wasn't callous. He took a little boy's pleasure in excitement and adventure that he couldn't contain. Shaving his wife's head seemed to have some of the same appeal.

I kept my eyes scrunched closed so I wouldn't have to watch, but I could feel the cool metal sailing over my skull. I clutched the arms of my chair. For such a little bit of hair, it took a long time. Daniel hummed as he worked. When I finally opened my eyes, I stared at myself in the mirror. There I was. Bald. I stared and stared, trying to find myself. I tried to pretend I was like the beautiful woman in the Taoist story who disfigured herself so she could reach enlightenment without distraction, but it was tough. I didn't want enlightenment; I wanted hair. I looked shrunken, more vulnerable, sick. I closed my eyes, hoping the whole scene would go away.

—

I WAS ONLY able to see Zev once or twice while in hospital, and I had to wear a mask and gown and gloves at those times. But I was happy that he was nestled in the care of his grandparents and aunts and uncles. My mom, Roberta, was Zev's primary caregiver and organized his care schedule. My sisters, Lori and Shelley, and their families bounced between caring for Zev and coming to the hospital to see me. Barbara and Leon came up from California to visit me and to help relieve my mother's load. Because of their distance from us, they rarely saw Zev and savoured this time with him.

Right up until the transplant, I had still been trying to be the perfect mother. I had fussed over Zev's diet and obsessed over his sleep schedule. At the beginning of my transplant I had tried to micromanage his care from hospital, but I soon had to abandon that strategy; it was an impossible task and made everyone cranky. I was feeling sick and needed to concentrate on getting through this ordeal. I had to trust everyone. I had to let go. The only important factor was that he was with someone who loved him. Everything else was gravy.

Regardless of who he was with, Zev seemed happy and unaware of my situation. He was like those travel electricity adapters. You could plug him in to any outlet, give him something to eat, and he would light up and be content.

20

DANIEL WAS OUT on a quest... in downtown Toronto ... in rush hour. It was, truly, a quest driven by love, as Toronto rush hour is not for the faint of heart or anyone actually in a rush. He was off in search of gnocchi with tomato cream sauce. For me.

My counts were beginning to climb, meaning my bone marrow was starting to kick in. When I had been without an immune system, my eating had been restricted to food prepared safely for my immune-deficient state and lovingly for my sensitive stomach. That meant, usually, chicken soup. It was really good chicken soup; my mother's homemade, that she cooked all night. She was desperate to nourish me. But by the time I hit the low point in the treatment, I couldn't even look at chicken soup.

By some coincidence, many of the books I had brought with me to read while in hospital had significant food components: a fancy banquet outlined, course by course, with the language and skill of a great food enthusiast; a diary of a restaurant reviewer who allowed me to vicariously experience the ethereal flavours of her favourite restaurants; and a sci-fi survivor cooking for herself from her rebuilt garden in that simple and casual way that rural Italians or French cook, relying on the flavours of the ingredients themselves to carry the meal. Each book raised new eating possibilities in my mind and stirred desire, even when I was at my most nauseated. As I started to feel better, I gained some appetite, but was finding the chicken soup anemic rather than comforting. Chicken soup was for sickness. I started dreaming about real food, food that was vibrant and had some moxie.

Daniel offered to go fetch me the food of my dreams the minute my doctor approved restaurant food. I put in a request for my ultimate comfort food, gnocchi in a tomato cream sauce from a particular restaurant in Toronto. I never made this easy. My family understood this comfort of food. We were a family of food lovers.

> April 27, 2016
> Dear Family,
>
> The weather forecast for Montreal this weekend is pleasant, but cold. As far as snacks, we'll all probably want to bring our own stuff. I am bringing cookies, a bag of roasted nuts, a cut-up apple, some buttered matzo, hard-boiled eggs, cut up tomatoes/cucumbers, celery and avocado and lots of napkins. I will also bring a small jar of dressing. I know it sounds like a lot, but we do have a few hours en route. I guess we can buy coffee, water etc. Let me know what you all think.

Before a family trip to Montreal to celebrate my mother's eightieth birthday, there was essential email correspondence between family members about food. My mother launched the discussion by sending out her eating plans for the five-hour train ride and was replied to in kind by the rest of the family.

In our family, you don't drive longer than an hour without considering what you should bring for snacks. No plans are made without considering the food angle and working out what the menu will be and who will be responsible (and are they up to the job?).

Our family language is food. Our family culture is food. We discuss current affairs and argue over politics, but eventually the discussion defaults to food. We travel to remote locations through hellish traffic to find that perfect ingredient. We use birthdays to buy novel kitchen gadgets for each other. If you phone any of us in the evening we are likely to be cooking, eating or washing up, as our meals are usually major affairs.

At times this emphasis on food can be a burden. Somehow, whenever I cook, I pick recipes that involve maximum chopping and a mountain of dishes. I didn't grow up learning how to "throw together" a quick dinner.

It isn't a foodie thing; our family is not devoted to fashion eating. Rather, we all have a desire to make food that tastes good and is comforting. We get pleasure from feeding others. We find joy in masterful flavours and will reminisce about favourite meals. Our devotion to food is both hedonistic and soul-giving.

At one point, my husband asked Zev what he had learned from us, his parents. He replied, "Save your money." My husband's family culture emphasizes saving and growing your money.

Zev considered a bit longer and then added, "But if you're going to spend your money, spend it on food."

—

THIS DEVOTION TO food has its roots in our ancestry. Eastern European Jewish blood, Ashkenazi blood, courses thickly through our veins. Generations of borscht-eating, Yiddish-speaking ancestors converge in my sisters and me, descending through all four of our grandparents whose families were part of the mass migration of Jews out of Eastern Europe in the late 1800s and early 1900s. Eastern European lips were passed on to me by my father and grandmother; full red lips that grew to adult size while I was still young. My red hair and green eyes descend through my mother's line.

Along with these physical features came a tradition of food that's notable enough to be familiar in the broader culture. Chopped liver, chicken soup, schmaltz and the traditional Jewish mother are well known to most from TV, movies and comedy routines.

My grandmother's parents lived in a small town in Russia, where my great-grandfather worked as the miller. There were only two Jewish families in that town, so when the Jewish holidays arrived, families would gather from all around to celebrate with my great-grandparents. The kitchen would fill with sturdy women hauling sacks and pots, who would clatter and chop and gossip as they cooked. They would have prepared food without recipes, perhaps disagreeing on the flavouring of the chicken soup or the fineness of the chopped liver. Gefilte fish, kasha, honey cake. The making of the food would have been as celebratory as the eating and would have nourished the spirits as much as the bodies of these women.

I think to my mother in her modern kitchen still making the traditional foods. She insists on using a hand-cranked food mill to make the chopped liver and only recently relented and allowed herself to use the food processor rather than a hand grater to make potato latkes. Her potato knishes take several days to make, in a multi-step process that involves the rendered chicken fat called *schmaltz*. Chopping,

frying, rolling, cutting, baking. Bite into one of these little gems and your teeth only have to press lightly to break
through the crumbly golden pastry on the outside into the
soft, heavenly filling made from mashed potatoes, onions,
chicken fat and other secret ingredients. This is peasant food
in all of its high-fat glory.

"Sam, the secret to making really good chicken soup is
to start with good chickens. It's best to use kosher chickens,
the yellow kind. And get a pullet—make sure it's a proper
pullet. Then you let it cook all night." This is how my mother
advises me on recreating the golden, flavour-dense ambrosia
that she conjures up in her kitchen. My childhood is filled
with memories of being lulled to sleep by the rich smell of
broth sneaking up the stairs and curling around my bed.

Sometimes I find myself marvelling at my mother as she
describes a traditional Jewish recipe. She dresses with style
and worked for years in advertising. She watches cooking
shows on the Food Network and is aware of the latest food
trends. But no amount of time in the slick and brisk world
of advertising or the modern TV food world has been able to
destroy the deeply embedded knowledge, skill and love necessary to make this chicken soup. It is part of her foundation.

My mother learned her art from her mother and mother-
in-law and then perfected her recipes through conversations
with other Jewish cooks and through her careful attention to
detail. I tried to document some of these recipes and each
one was pages long, filled with addendums that captured all
that she had learned over the years. And as we worked our way
through each dish, I realized that these recipes were our living history, passed down mother to daughter to grandchild. I
could see, I could *feel* my great-grandmother turning the food
mill. I could see and smell her neighbour chopping onions.

We were akin. My love of food, the great comfort I take from food, has a source that is generations old. When something is so foundational in your life, it's not easy to toss aside.

—

IN THE DAYS leading up to what I called my "big eat," it was all I could do to not spend every waking minute anticipating that first bite. It was excruciating waiting for the final approval from the medical team to eat restaurant food. Gnocchi with a tomato cream sauce was a superlative dish. The gnocchi were a heavenly marriage of potatoes and flour, formed into tight, satisfying packages that went down with silky smoothness. They were marked with grooves to allow maximum delivery of the over-the-top tomato sauce that contained enough cream to make you weak in the knees, but not flatten you. The grated parmesan sprinkled on top provided a salty, gritty contrast to the creaminess of the sauce and the silkiness of the gnocchi.

On the big day, Daniel set off to face Toronto traffic while I waited in my room, counting down the time and setting up my table for some serious eating. He returned after an hour and a half, triumphant with his booty. I opened the container and gazed at the pasta with love, savouring the moment of eating. The hospital room and my recent ordeal of the transplant receded as I beheld this symbol of a normal life, a life outside the hospital, a life where the sensuousness of food could be celebrated.

A meal could transform a moment or even a whole day for me. And now I was about to re-enter the world of full-on eating and days of richness and colour. It was the moment of truth. I took a bite and waited for the flavour of the warm, creamy river of sauce to take over my mouth. But it didn't. I kept chewing and waiting, but there was no flavour. The more I chewed, the more it felt like I was trying to eat lumps of gluey playdough. I finally got it down and turned to Daniel, who had been watching me with an expectant smile that was now fading as he saw my face.

"It tastes like cardboard, Daniel. I might as well eat the container." And then I couldn't hold back the tears. "What if it's like this forever?"

The chemo destroyed all rapidly reproducing cells. That included the diseased cells, but it also included hair follicles and cells in my digestive tract and my mouth. My taste buds had gone AWOL. No one had warned me that food would become something to endure rather than enjoy.

21

From: Roberta Albert
Monday, November 20, 2000
Subject: Progress Report

Hello to all,

SAM CAME HOME FROM THE HOSPITAL YESTERDAY!

It was very exciting, emotional and heart-warming to have her walk in the front door, looking radiant (yes radiant) in her exotic turban, flushed with the momentousness of the occasion and the happiness she was feeling. It was especially touching to see her with Zev...

...She tires quickly but is feeling well. And Zev won't leave her alone, which has been her greatest delight. She was convinced he would not know her after this length of time and the number of caregivers he has had. But there he was, clinging to her at every opportunity. There was not a dry eye in the house...

Roberta

Daniel helped me up the stairs of my mother's condo and Barbara and Leon came behind carrying all the flotsam from my hospital room. I took a breath and opened the door, trying not to have any hopes for this reunion. Zev was only two and he'd hardly seen me the last two weeks. Zev and my mom were sitting with a book and my mom called out, "Zev, look who it is! It's Mama." At first, he seemed intent on finishing the book. As I came closer, and he saw it was me, however, he put out his arms for me to pick him up. I wrapped him in my embrace as tightly as I could, my head falling over his shoulder, whispering into his ear.

"Oh, you're such a beautiful boy, you're so wonderful. I've missed you so much. I love you so much." Over and over again I whispered these sweet nothings and felt myself relax into the curve of his body. Usually, he would squirm away from such a hug, but this day he was patient with my need to squeeze him tight and feel his heartbeat and hear his breath. I don't know who needed this more.

What if I hadn't made it? Daniel was with Zev every night and morning and Zev had become used to me being away while I had prepared for the transplant. Our family members who had looked after him while I was in hospital all reported a happy child. Yet that first hug told me he understood something momentous was going on; something you embraced and didn't squirm away from. Would he have known if I'd died? Would he have remembered me? Would he have felt the hole in his life? How does he even understand "mother" in his mind? How does he know it's me?

I put Zev down and watched him toddle a tour around the room. Feeling weak, I took a seat on a large chair and watched his progress. He came back to me holding *The Very Hungry Caterpillar* and plopped down in what I had of a lap, demanding that I read. Daniel followed him and squeezed in beside me.

"Here we are," I said, giving Daniel a kiss. "Together again."

PART FIVE

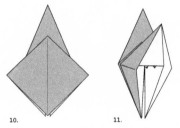

10.   11.

22

TAP, TAP, TAP.

I was glued to the couch.

Tap, tap, tap. I felt little pricks on my nose.

I flashed my eyes open to find a pair of big blue eyes staring right into mine.

"Mama, Mama, play!" Two-year-old Zev stood beside the couch, hanging over me, a dinosaur dangling from his hand.

"A few more minutes, sweetie, and then Mama will play. Mama's very tired." I closed my eyes and was asleep again almost instantly.

There was an explosion by my ear that caused me to sit up quickly, my heart pounding, a curse caught behind my lips. I didn't manage to hide the snarl of frustration that flashed across my face before Zev saw it. His lower lip wobbled.

"Mama, play," he said in a woeful tone, his toy drum now abandoned beside the couch.

"Oh, honey, come here." I reached for him and he snuggled into my arms. I inhaled his sweet smell; a combination of toddler sweat, baby powder and the tomato sauce from lunch. I held him tight and rocked him. I should have been making cookies and playing with him and taking him to museums and on nature walks. Instead, I was catatonic on the couch and testy when he wanted me to actually do something. I sighed and hugged him closer.

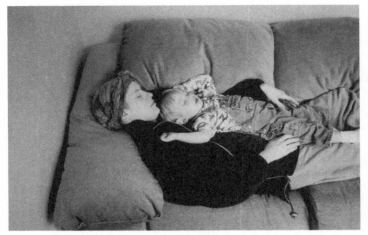

Zev and I asleep on the couch, in the exhausting period after my stem-cell transplant

I turned Zev to face me and put my forehead up to his, "You surprised me, that's all. I'm not angry. Why don't you choose a book and we can curl up and read it together?" He squirmed away from me, leaving a cold, hollow place, and said, "No. Play, Mama."

My sweet boy grinned at me and tugged at my hand. He was restored and I was forgiven. But my limbs were still made of lead. I roused myself the best I could. Zev produced a dump truck and ran it back and forth, loading and unloading dinosaurs. I deposited a few token dinosaurs before leaning back on the couch to watch through slit eyes as Zev vroomed them around the room. Like a hummingbird, he would only sit down for a moment before he was up again, running as much as he could within the confines of our living room. Sometimes he would pause at one of the baby gates. For a moment, he would be very still looking out at the vast worlds in the other rooms. Reason #753 to feel guilty.

Finally, he settled down to play with his stacking blocks. The next thing I knew, I was waking to the sound of Daniel coming in through the door. A jerk of my arm knocked over some of Zev's blocks. He whimpered while I sat there dazed, wiping drool off my face and trying to figure out what time it was.

Daniel came rushing in at the sound of Zev's tears and picked him up.

"Hey, little bean, it's okay. What's going on?" Zev sniffled into his shoulder.

Daniel pointed his nose at Zev's behind and said, "Oh, my friend, you are in need of a new diaper. No wonder you're unhappy." Daniel didn't mean it as a reproach, but it still felt like a cut. I didn't even get a kiss hello. He whisked our boy upstairs and I could hear horse noises and Zev giggling. He hadn't giggled all day with me; I only made him cry.

I retreated to our bedroom and listened as Daniel cooked dinner and entertained Zev. They made the kitchen seem like a warm and cozy place to be, while I was alone in the cold bedroom.

I'd survived the hardships of the treatment and was now free of the hospital. This time should have felt like a victory lap. Instead, I felt like the Roadrunner's Coyote after being flattened by a falling anvil. Unlike Coyote, I seemed incapable of peeling myself up off of the pavement and popping out to full size. I was bald, thin and exhausted, with a fatigue that was debilitating and depressing.

Later that night, I leaned into Daniel and he held me and rocked me as I cried.

"Sam, it will get better. It's only been a short time. I know it's hard." He was silent for a few moments. Then he spoke over the top of my head.

"But I do think we need some help. Why don't we look into daycare?" I pulled away to look at him.

"But I'm not even working."

"Don't you think it will be better for Zev to be with playmates and people who have the energy to look after him?"

My tears started afresh. We had always planned to put Zev in daycare so I could work. But putting him in while I was home seemed wrong somehow, as if I wasn't trying hard enough.

I caught sight of myself in the mirror. My head scarf had slipped off and my thin face looked skeletal without any hair. I felt ugly and pathetic and useless. How could I even pretend to parent Zev right now? All I could do was warehouse him while I napped. I was failing at mothering.

This was a period filled with waiting. Waiting for restored strength, waiting for hair, waiting for blood counts that would show me "cured," waiting to see what would be next for me. The verdict was still out on the success of the treatment.

"Okay," I said in a hoarse voice. "For Zev."

———

I DROPPED ZEV off for his first day at the new daycare, smiling at the brightly coloured decorations on the wall, the plethora of toys and the happy hum of other children. This would be a good place for him to spend his days. He held my hand as he tottered around looking at the sights.

We'd visited here once together, and I'd tried to explain to him what daycare meant, but I wasn't sure he understood that I would be leaving. Not that I wasn't away a great deal, but this was different; this was a room full of strangers, not friends or family.

I kissed and hugged him goodbye, reassured him that I would see him at the end of the day and walked out of the room, clutching my purse as if it was one of his stuffed toys.

I stopped outside of the door with my head against the wall and listened to his wails at my departure. I thought that I must surely be the worst mother, to be taking my child to daycare when I wasn't even working. I had betrayed him. He did stop crying after a long time. I continued to stand there undecided, too tired and heavy to move. Eventually I turned for home.

At the end of the day I was prepared to tell the daycare that Zev needed to be home with me. But when I arrived, he was happily engaged in hammering on a bright plastic table. No tears. No remonstrative looks. No resentment. Content.

After that first day, he would strain to get out of the car when we arrived, eager to be inside the daycare. He couldn't wait to see his friends, discover the new toys of the day and participate in snack. It was with mixed feelings that I realized how replaceable I was.

23

MY HAIR STARTED to grow back. First that hopeful fuzz, like the haze of green on trees in the early spring. With each passing day, I examined my scalp and could see the hair sprouting. The new hair was wiry and hinted at curls. Daniel couldn't stop bouncing his hand on my springy head. "At least I got curls out of it!" I would say of the transplant.

When I felt that I was ready to launch into the world without the security of a head scarf, we had a coming out party for my hair. It would be my first appearance *sans scarf*. I invited my friends, my family, my tai chi community; all who had provided such profound support throughout a very unbalanced time in our lives. I was celebrating not only the re-emergence of my hair, but the re-emergence of my life. Having hair signified an end to the recovery period of my transplant and I wanted to mark the moment with a celebration.

A crowd squeezed into our little house and a deep feeling of gratitude welled up as I wandered through the party offering up hors d'oeuvres. "No, I'm happy, these are happy tears." We had turned the corner and I was making my comeback. Now it was time to get ready to go back to work.

—

"MAY I HELP you?" I looked up and saw a saleswoman with long black shiny hair approaching us. She was dressed in a sleek blue suit with a tasteful, low-cut blouse. I squirmed in my sweatpants and tai chi T-shirt and rubbed my hand over my newly populated head.

"We're looking for a suit. For her. And she's very picky." My mother's long finger pointed at me. I felt about twelve.

"Nothing fancy," I interjected before my mother had me going home in something with shoulder pads. "A classic pant suit that's not going to go out of style tomorrow."

I had my first consulting job lined up and when I mentioned to my mom that I didn't have work clothes that fit anymore, she had insisted on taking me to Tom's, the discount designer suit store in Toronto, to buy me a real suit. With my gaunt face surrounded by a bristling of hair and a belly inflated to the size of a five-months-pregnant woman, I wanted a smashing outfit that would give me the confidence to walk into my first contract and feel that I belonged.

My only previous experience at a suit store was helping Daniel select his wedding outfit at Harry Rosen's, a high-end chain store. That quiet, gilded store made us feel as if we should whisper. Salesmen glided to their refined customers and spoke in well-modulated tones. The suits were tastefully displayed on minimalist racks.

Tom's, on the other hand, a Toronto tradition since the 50s, was raucous with kibitzing, gossip and heated negotiations over price. It felt more like a family gathering than a business. The suits were crammed into racks and the racks were jammed up next to each other separated by tiny paths, as if it was a hoarder's lair.

I looked out over the sea of suits in the women's section with some despair. How many would I have to try on? But I had underestimated the saleswoman. After warming me up with two failures, she handed me a slim, iron-grey suit. I put it on, and the blazer fit cleverly to hide my belly. The pants didn't quite do up, but the cut of the legs was perfect. In this suit, my short, short hair looked hip. My head looked right. I looked like a professional.

"What do you think?" my mother asked the saleswoman.

"*I* think it's great," I squeaked out. My mother nodded absently and waited to hear a pronouncement from the saleswoman.

"I agree with your daughter. It's the perfect look."

"Can you alter this?" my mother asked, lifting up the blazer and showing the pants. "She's having an operation and needs this to fit around the belly."

I looked a question at my mom, who avoided my eyes as she looked through more suits. When the saleswoman walked over to talk to someone else, I turned to my mother and asked, "An operation?" I don't know why it bothered me so much, but I felt that I should be telling people an accurate rendition of what was happening, not making stuff up.

My mother shrugged. "It's easier to explain that way." Still not looking at me.

I stood staring at my mom. I saw the hardness of her jaw, the lines around her eyes, the pursed mouth. What must it be like to have to discuss your daughter's life-threatening illness or her distorted body with a stranger? I let it go.

———

MY DOCTOR ANALYZED my blood work, drumming his fingers on the table. I knew the top of his head well; the whorls of light-brown hair that never altered in their precision.

"How are you feeling?" He spoke to the paper.

"Getting better, feeling stronger."

"Mmhmmm." He kept looking at the paper.

"Your test results are stable."

I waited for more.

"Well, we'll continue to watch you. Come back to see me in three months." He stood up, ready to move on to the next patient.

"Uh, so where are we at? What can I expect now? "

He sat back down and actually looked at me. But there was no warmth in the look. There was something else—his eyes were studying me rather than connecting with me. Was it curiosity? Amusement? Impatience? I wasn't sure, but from the way he perched on his chair I could tell he was eager to move on.

"Well, the disease is controlled . . . for now."

"For now?"

"For now. We talk about functional cures now for amyloidosis instead of a permanent cure."

"So, at any time I could get worse again?"

"Yes. But we'll watch you. Anything else?" I shook my head and he made his escape.

I packed up my things and wandered into the atrium, squinting at the bright sun and leaning on the railing that looked over the lobby.

For now. It was as if someone had led me to sit on the top of a volcano and said, "You should be okay *for now.* It might or might not erupt. If it erupts, it could be tomorrow or next week or in fifty years. For the moment it's not erupting, so you're safe."

I had thought the stem-cell transplant was a permanent cure. And if the transplant didn't work, we would try the next treatment and the next, until we had found the one that would cure my illness. This was the first I had heard of, or at least the first time that my brain had registered, the term "functional cure" in relation to my illness. The stem-cell transplant had been endurable because I could envision my life on the other side as being free of illness. But after this meeting, it was clear that I would never be free of illness. Even if I experienced no symptoms for the next fifty years, I would still be on the edge of that volcano, imagining the molten rock, ash and steam bursting through the earth's crust and creating a hot river of destruction.

—

BUT FOR NOW, at least, I had hair and I had a suit. Zev was in a great daycare. Recovery had been slow and sad; each day had to be endured and survived. The days were becoming a cut above endurable. I could do more. I was ready and eager to get back to work and back on track with our future; to regain my "normal" life. Except I wasn't really sure what that "normal" life was. Between interruptions for schooling, adventures, having Zev and then getting sick, I'd never worked for more than a year in any one serious job. My career path was more like a deer trail than a highway. What would I do with my life?

I decided I wanted to keep working in community development, but not alone and not for an organization. My friend and I formed a loose network of community development professionals who liked to perform complementary tasks. That way, when one of us landed a contract, we could pull others in, flexibly, to help with specific parts of a project.

My friend in this network landed us a big contract developing volunteer resources for rural organizations. We pulled together our team, a group of six talented women. I attended meetings, facilitated workshops and wrote copy. I enjoyed the work, the camaraderie, the feeling of contributing to the household income. What freedom to go a whole day without talking about my blood counts or my bowel movements. I had purpose again. I was doing work that I felt mattered in the world. When I went to parties, I had something to say when I was, inevitably, asked what it was I did.

The next months were filled with activity and optimism. My colleagues and I did high-quality work for our contracts and were already discussing future projects. We were getting noticed, we were on a roll. Daniel's business, while demanding, was blossoming (pardon the pun) in our garden-crazy city. People loved his designs and his gentle manner. I was still practicing and teaching tai chi, but somehow it all felt manageable. Both Daniel and Zev were happier now that I was doing well and had more energy. My ability to make dinner, play with Zev or go to the grocery store felt like a wonder to me. We had entered a golden period. We could breathe our collective sigh and carry on where we left off.

I'd like to freeze the story right here; move right into the happily-ever-after. But, of course, it didn't work that way.

PART SIX

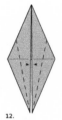

12.

13.

24

THE RAINDROPS HIT the windshield with staccato plops to accompany the thumping *swish swash* of the wipers. The rhythm lulled me as I drove, fuelling my fatigue. I could hold it together until I got home, but just barely. My body ached for a nap.

A small voice called out from the backseat.

"Mama," said four-year-old Zev. "When we get home let's play dinosaurs!"

I sagged. "Oh sweetie, Mama needs to take a nap when we get home. Remember Mama's sick and needs to rest a lot."

I could see Zev's face in the rearview mirror as he looked out at a passing truck. He sat in his booster throne, regal and confident. When he turned to the front again, his blue eyes met mine.

"Papa's more fun than you are, Mama." And he turned back to look out the window again.

The words travelled to the pit of my stomach and stung.

"Yes sweetie, Papa is more fun than me. Aren't we lucky to have him as a papa?" I looked in the rearview mirror again, but Zev was still absorbed by something outside.

I slowed to a stop for the red light at our street, and waited, tapping the steering wheel.

"Yes. I love Papa more than I love you, Mama." He took a drink from his sippy cup.

My stomach now turned into a hard knot. I blinked hard. The sound of the traffic around me receded. In the silence, I listened to the pounding beat of the wipers echoing the pounding in my ears. Water beaded on the windshield. The black rubber dragged on the glass.

The light changed and I turned onto our street, my hands stretched white around the steering wheel.

"What's for dinner, Mama?"

—

IT WAS THREE years post-transplant and my health was unravelling. A debilitating fatigue had returned. The work of which I had been so proud had become a burden to finish with limited energy. I signed off on the project and retired to my couch.

My doctor restaged me. I was immersed once again into the medical diagnostic world and asked to drink, fast, hold my breath, collect pee, etc. Finally, I had a follow-up appointment, my sister Shelley by my side, my doctor holding test results in hand.

"Well, it looks like the stem-cell transplant only had a limited benefit," said the doctor to his paper, and then to Shelley, "We need to look at other treatment options."

If the stem-cell-transplant hadn't worked, what else could I do? What if nothing worked? There was a thrumming in my chest as I listened to him speak.

Still talking to my sister, the doctor said, "The studies show that a combination of oral chemotherapy, high-dose prednisone and thalidomide are effective in controlling the disease."

Thalidomide? Thalidomide babies popped into my mind. I thought that drug was destroyed and banned forever from the planet. And he was suggesting that I take it?

"I don't feel that comfortable taking thalidomide," I said, trying to sound assertive instead of like a scared little kid.

The doctor looked over at me. He took a moment to consider and then, as if he had made some kind of a decision, said, "Well then, we could start with the oral chemo and the prednisone and go from there."

I was surprised that he agreed without much hesitation. But I guessed that it wasn't critical if he wasn't trying to persuade me. Shelley didn't say anything, so we left it at that.

He wrote the prescriptions, arranged for follow-up and was gone.

———

AT THAT TIME, many friends my age were having second and third babies, moving on to better jobs, real grown-up jobs in their field. They were building businesses, writing books and living in exotic places like Mongolia and Sierra Leone. One was staying home to teach her child; another was teaching on a boat that sailed the world.

I was going to doctors' appointments, enduring medical procedures, waiting for blood test results. I was hanging my happiness on my alkaline phosphatase, creatinine, hemoglobin and other numbers in my blood work that I had little control over. I napped. I practiced as much tai chi as I could and I fumbled through housework. Daniel, once again, had to add so many more responsibilities to a schedule that was already impossible. Zev was in daycare full-time, but I had little energy for him when he was home. I was incapable of fulfilling any of my roles except that of patient.

When I was asked the inevitable "What do you do?" at a party, I would shrug and mumble my response. I was stuck in mud, flailing to get out, while everyone else appeared to be carrying on down the path.

25

AFTER A YEAR of dragging myself around and seeing only minimal changes from the chemo–prednisone combination, my doctor said to me, "You know, we would probably see better results if we could add thalidomide."

I was ready to give in to his suggestion, any suggestion. The last year had been one of continued fatigue. My liver had grown enough that several times I had been asked if I was pregnant. I was ready to try whatever he wanted me to try. I wanted to feel better. I wanted a smaller liver. He had worn me down into a compliant patient.

Before I could get my prescription, I was required to take a pregnancy test. I presented myself to the local blood lab, handing the requisition to the technician.

"I'm here for a pregnancy test," I told her, thrusting my belly out.

She stared at me, her mouth opening slightly, frozen in a tableau of confusion.

Finally, she collected herself, "Go sit in chair number 4. I'll be right there."

—

I BROUGHT THE little white pill bottles home from the hospital and studied them. I couldn't believe I was going to take this infamous drug.

"This is the moment when I begin to take thalidomide," I thought to myself.

My life would be divided into BT and AT.

I took the pill and waited. It wasn't rational, but I expected drama. Maybe I'd sprout a tail or grow some horns. The first day was uneventful. Second day, uneventful. By the end of the first week, I was popping these pills with all the rest.

I went for blood tests every few weeks and each test showed steady improvement in the course of my disease. The thalidomide was actually controlling my illness.

—

THE PREDNISONE, THALIDOMIDE and cyclophospha-mide (a chemo drug) were the first pebbles of an avalanche of other medications. Those three were the main treatment medications. Then there were drugs for the side effects. Sometimes there were even drugs for the side effects of the side-effects drugs. I needed a drug to help with my liver function and another to help with the restless legs I had developed. The amyloid was giving me severe heartburn, requiring yet another medication.

In the early days, I resisted every new medication. How toxic was it? Did I really need it? The "factsheets" that accompanied each one didn't help. As I read these sheets it was easy to imagine that I would experience all of the listed side effects.

My doctor told me that the oral chemotherapy he was pre-scribing (to treat my cancer-like illness) could cause cancer. Thus, my choice was to die then or possibly die in ten years. We gave Zev choices like that: "You can go to bed now or in five minutes." I wanted to ask for more choices.

I thought back to the day when my doctor first brought up thalidomide and I had a gut reaction to this notorious drug. Why did he give in so easily? Why didn't he take the time to talk to me and ease my fears? His job was to give me full information for making educated decisions. I could have had a different kind of year had I started thalidomide earlier; my liver may not have grown so large. I accept responsibility for making that choice, but had he spent more time with me, I might have changed my mind. Why didn't he do his job?

—

DANIEL GRABBED MY purse for me as we left the movie theatre. He gave it a shake.

"Boy, this is heavy. No wonder you're tired all the time. What do you have in here? What's that rattle?" He opened the purse and extracted a bottle full of a mix of pills.

"What's this for?"

"Well, it's just for emergencies."

"That's a lot of pills, Sam."

"Well, you just never know. If I was trapped somewhere in a snowstorm I wouldn't want to be without certain pills."

This was only partially true. The real reason I carried this stash of pills came from reading *Bel Canto*, the gorgeous book about a hostage-taking and an opera singer by Ann Patchett. I imagined myself in that situation, held hostage for days, maybe weeks. What would I do without my medication? In particular, I was told that I might go into shock or experience tremendous withdrawal if I suddenly stopped taking the high-dose prednisone.

I saw myself trapped in a dark room, tied to a chair, convulsing violently because my prednisone had been cut off. The kidnappers would panic when they saw my convulsions and not know what to do.

"Prednisone," I would croak out, but since they likely would be from a foreign country (kidnapping me for state secrets) they wouldn't understand, and I would finally die of my withdrawal only moments before a deal was struck with my government.

I only carried a week's worth of pills. I counted on the kidnappers to negotiate quickly.

—

I WAS IN my mid-thirties when I purchased my first pill organizer; those plastic containers with slots for each day of the week. I had held out because I felt too young to own one, but the complexity of my illness forced my hand.

My pill regime fluctuated over the years, but it was always full and complex. This is a sample of one moment in time.

Daily:

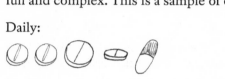

Morning:

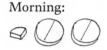

Evening:

Take these before bed, an hour away from eating dairy:

Every four hours:

Three times a day with food:

Once a week add:

On an as-needed basis add:

For three weeks out of four, add: every night. In addition
to the pills, there is an injectable drug, a cream and a puffer.

I became a skilled manager of the intricacies of my medications. It was no small job and it never let up. I came to
brandish my pill organizer with pride. I had earned it.

—

ONCE A WEEK I would sit down with my shoebox overflowing with medication and my pill organizer. Urso, Mirapex,
Atarax, calcitriol, Pariet and on and on, filed neatly into their
slots. It reminded me of those sorting games that toddlers
are invited to play while educators assess their skills. I had
done well on this kindergarten task. I would have received
a gold star on this new sorting activity had those educators
been watching.

Zev was fascinated by my ritual of pill sorting and taking. I could understand why the sorting might have seemed
interesting, with the pills of assorted shapes, colours and
sizes, some of them bright as jewels. I guess there was also
some entertainment value in watching me take my pills. I
would put one in my mouth and do a funny little head movement that Zev later described as looking akin to a penguin
preparing food in its gullet before serving it back to its chick.

One day, when he was five, he sat with me as I did my sorting, watching with a focused intensity. After I had downed my first pill, he jumped up and said, "Wait, wait!" and ran out of the room. A moment later he came in clutching a box of red, cinnamon Tic Tacs. He poured one into his hand and said, "Okay. Ready." As I took my next pill, he put the Tic Tac on his tongue, did a caricature of my own penguin-parent head motion and swallowed. He stuck his tongue out as far as he could to show me his empty mouth. Tic Tac all gone.

26

"HONEY, YOU ARE all in the belly."
I turned to find a hotel concierge standing next to me, her gaze fixed upon my belly.

"Pardon?"

"You're all in the belly!" She moved her gaze up from my belly to my face and grinned. "Me, when I was pregnant, I was in the hips and in the ass. But you are all... in... the... belly." Each word punctuated her amazement.

My smile was polite, but I needed to escape or change the subject. I spied her name tag.

"Jessica, I wonder if you could tell me about..." but another concierge walked by and Jessica shouted out to her,

"Yolanda! Come here a sec. Isn't she all in the belly?"

Yolanda ambled over, looked me up and down like a particularly interesting cut of meat and nodded, saying, "Uh-huh, a-a-all in the belly." The *a* in *all* sounded like its own word the way she stretched it out. I was now completely trapped under their gazes, wishing to be anywhere else.

At last, the elevator arrived and Jessica and I stepped in, waving goodbye to Yolanda. As we rose to the upper floors, Jessica continued to grin and bob her head, muttering "All in the belly!" looking as if she was the proud mama herself. After much smiling and bobbing of my own I made an escape at the fourth floor.

"Enjoy your stay in Philadelphia," she called after me.

I closed the door to my hotel room and sank into a chair. Me and my liver could relax. We'd survived another belly spotting.

—

I ALREADY KNEW my liver was special, but its uniqueness was brought home while lying one day under the lengthy examination of a new doctor. The blue hospital gown was soft and well worn, but the paper on the table had a sharp, crinkly, edgy feel. The doctor finally stopped his examination and looked at me.

"I have some medical students out there," he wheedled, pointing through the door, "and they may never see a liver like this again. Would you mind if they came in to take a look?"

With two sisters who had gone through medical school, I understood the need to support this educational moment. I will admit that I also didn't mind being a bit of a celebrity, even if it was for my giant liver. In came three students, which felt about right for the room. But then two more came in, chatting, followed by a rush of four more. I expected them to keep flowing in as if we were in a clown car full of doctors. Finally, they settled down and the doctor described my case and chose two lucky students to examine my liver.

New doctors that I meet take an obvious pleasure in palpating my liver, a process that involves extensive tapping to find the edges and quality of the organ. A normal, healthy liver mostly hides behind the ribs, with a small part hanging down below. It can be a challenge to palpate. My liver is a palpator's heaven. It's twice as long as a normal liver, bigger than a football, extending down to the base of my abdomen and reaching across my belly to meet up with my enlarged spleen. There is no hiding such a liver.

—

WHEN I WAS pregnant with Zev, I had been delighted that my belly was the centre of attention, receiving the coos of friends, family and strangers. I would stroke the large mound and feel for signs of emerging life. Having always felt scrawny, I admired my new heft and enhanced breasts in the mirror with satisfaction.

One of the manifestations of the amyloidosis was an enlarged liver that shaped my body into a cruel parody of my earlier pregnant self. I felt as if my body was an optical illusion, like the picture that can be seen either as a candlestick or two faces depending on how you view it. If you looked at me and thought "pregnant woman," beautiful images might come to mind of cradling a newborn, holding tiny hands between giant-size palms or feeling the warmth of a small child in your lap. Most bellies that looked like mine signified new life and were accompanied by an optimism about the future, draped with the hopes and dreams of the parents. A wanted baby was a reason for celebration and could transform a family.

If you refocused your eyes, however, and let the jarring reality hit you that a liver filled out my abdomen instead of a baby, those beautiful images dissolved and distorted into something ugly and diseased. My belly signified death and the loss of hope. Who would want to celebrate that?

—

THE YOUNG MAN at the Japanese fast-food place swirled the mop around with amazing, ineffective vigour, missing great swaths of floor as he eyed me. Finally, he came and leaned in close over me, his hair flopping over one eye.

"I'm going to guess seven months."

"Pardon me?" I said, pulling back from his enthusiasm.

"I guess that you're seven months along."

"Uh... that's amazing, how did you know?"

"I took a course on this and I did really well. I know a lot about this."

I smiled at him and considered how to respond.

"Excellent guessing," I said. He smiled back, stood up and returned to his mopping with a little hop-skip motion.

If I had wanted to be technically accurate, I should have said that I was about one hundred and thirty-two months along. But I would have spoiled his moment by offering the truth. Besides, he was no amateur. I subsequently verified my size by standing next to women of different pregnant states. This young man knew his stuff. When needed, I would be seven months pregnant.

—

"C'MON SAM AND Zev, the line is moving," Daniel called out to us. He was holding our place in the slow airport line while I entertained seven-year-old Zev from a resting position. Zev jumped up and pulled me to my feet when he heard his dad's announcement. We gathered our bits and pieces and joined Daniel in the line of tourists returning to winter after their Cancun vacations. I held Zev's hand as the line moved; this was too big a crowd to get lost in.

As we finally approached a counter, I put my free hand behind my back and tried to add a subtle waddle to my walk. I wanted to reinforce the impression that already existed. With luck, my supposed pregnancy would get us the bulkhead seats on the crowded plane. I may not have been pregnant, but I was still big.

In the early days of my illness, I had been one-hundred-percent honest about my condition with anyone who asked. But I soon found that when I revealed my illness to those with whom I had fleeting contact I would leave distress in my wake. Crying salespeople, horrified grandmothers, embarrassed receptionists. It seemed kinder to nod and smile and take the offered chair or the special treat. Sometimes I even felt justified in receiving the occasional perk as mild recompense for a lifetime of illness.

We closed in on the ticket agent's counter, fluttering passports and tickets. Zev swung his foot back and forth as he hung off my arm. The ticket agent looked at me and asked, "And how far along are you, Ms. Albert?"

I was entranced by his musical Spanish accent and his thick black moustache.

"Seven months," I answered without a hiccup, trying to guess how much time he spent on maintaining his facial hair.

His mouth puckered up in distress, making the moustache twitch.

"Oh, Ms. Albert, I'm so sorry, but I cannot let you fly so late in your pregnancy."

I looked at the agent, trying to process his statement while pulling Zev firmly onto his feet. Daniel moved in to pick up our worried little boy and entertain him while I dealt with this situation.

"Is Mama going to have stay in Cancun?" I heard him ask as they walked away.

The agent looked at me, waiting, nostrils flaring with this unexpected complication. As I considered my options, I heard the couple at the kiosk next to me arguing over where they should sit, I heard a flight announcement over the loudspeaker, I heard Zev's giggle. I could get upset and blame the airline for not stopping me in Toronto and allowing me to be stranded in Mexico. I could cry and plead mercy. Finally, I took a breath, looked the ticket agent straight in the eye and said,

"Well, I'm not actually pregnant."

The agent looked me up and down with questioning eyes.

"I look pregnant, but I have this weird disease that makes my liver huge."

His eyes narrowed as he looked back at my face. I held out my Medic Alert bracelet, the only proof that I had.

"You see; it says here I've got a big liver." *Hepatomegaly.*

He didn't bother to look. His moustache twitched again.

"But you told me you were pregnant."

"Well, I'm not really pregnant. It's easier to explain pregnancy than a big liver." I tried to make my belly smaller.

Zev whined, "Mama, I have to pee."

The agent glared and handed us our boarding passes. No bulkhead seating.

—

IF I'M OUT and about, visiting new places, I may be asked three or four times in a day about my non-existent baby. Double that if I'm at a party with people I haven't met before. If I didn't have to, I wouldn't be broadcasting my story to the world; the belly forces me to.

How often do you make a new acquaintance only to have them say in the first five minutes, "I have colon cancer, you know?" or "Let me tell you about my leukemia." Yet I am having this conversation with perfect strangers almost every time I venture out. The questions, the assumptions, the pronouncements and the reactions create a wave of relentless force. One of the greatest joys of my online degree in creative writing was that none of the other students could see me. It was a belly-free zone.

In the early days of my illness, the pregnancy question was a sharp reminder of my non-pregnancy and the grief over our inability to have any more children. I didn't blame the people who asked me; there was no getting around the fact that I looked pregnant. But it was tiring and saddening to face it over and over again.

As I became resigned to life without a second child, I was less affected by the question. In fact, I almost relished some of the absurdities to add to my collection of stories. Like the waiter in the Chinese restaurant who spoke Cantonese baby talk to my liver or the furnace repairman who thought I was having a baby every year. Now that I am over fifty, the mistake feels more complimentary; someone thinks I'm still young enough to be bearing children. Sweet!

No, it's not the questions that cause me angst these days, but the responses. When people learn the truth, there is a visible moment of reorientation, a shifting of gears. Processing can be slow, and part of that processing is deciding how to react to me. This is a palpable moment, suspended in the air between the two of us. I dread where it might land. For it's easy to suddenly see me as the "other." I become a source of embarrassment or an object of interest, fear, anxiety or pity, even though less than five minutes earlier we were simply connecting, human to human.

My best strategy is to lug the discussion forward and hope that I can pull us past this pothole back onto a smooth road of conversation. Yes, people might look at me through a new filter after they find out the truth, but my hope is that they will not lose the sense of me, the person inside, the person independent of her belly who stands in front of them.

In those best cases, we can leave my belly behind and move forward in our connection. In other scenarios, people might back off, find excuses to leave or become overly cheerful to mask their discomfort.

Illness is a lonely journey at the best of times. I spend a great deal of time trapped in medical settings or at home. I am nourished, of course, by my close friends and family. But I am also fed by my interactions with the world at large, whether it's smiling to a stranger on the street or having meaningful encounters with new acquaintances. Connecting with others is a basic part of who I am. But my body precedes me as a herald of my illness, often foiling my efforts at connection, leaving me lonelier than when I was home alone. My belly has much to answer for.

—

"IS THERE A baby in your belly?" asked seven-year-old Alex, a young acquaintance at our family camp. His big brown eyes were earnest; he needed to know. One of his shoelaces was untied and I crouched down to tie it.

"No honey. I look pregnant. But I'm not. I have a really big liver."

Nothing changed on Alex's countenance to indicate either grief, horror or pity. It was simple information. He considered.

"Polar bears must really love you," he said with a big grin as I stood up.

"Why is that?"

"Because..." the grin spread to fill his entire face. He could barely contain his excitement. "... polar bears really like to eat liver."

Alex looked surprised and a bit annoyed when I pulled him in for a hug, but I didn't detain him long. As he ran off to tell his parents about polar bears, I let my laughter explode and wiped the tears from my face.

27

"WHEN ARE YOU due?" the clerk at the local discount store asked me, smiling.

"My mama's not pregnant." The clerk looked down at seven-year-old Zev, who was smiling up at her.

"No?" she said.

"No." Zev was standing tall with the importance of his task. I had not asked him to speak for me but was delighted to have him take over.

"She has a big liver." This was Zev's favourite part. "A really big liver." He pulled his hands away from each other as if he was demonstrating the size of the fish that got away. The clerk looked at me and I smiled and nodded. She looked back to Zev, confused.

"But she's fine!" Zev assured her. The clerk looked at me again and I nodded again.

"He's got it all right," I said.

She looked at Zev's smiling face and shrugged her shoulders as she finished ringing in our order.

I began to call Zev my belly ambassador. He was a buffer between me and the emotional responses of others. When Zev informed people of my liver in such a matter-of-fact manner, others were able to accept the new information about me and move on.

—

THE EARLY YEARS of Zev's life were filled with intense emotions as we navigated through my illness and our relationship: panic, anger, guilt, sadness and fear. We were under an inordinate amount of pressure.

But no matter how difficult it was between us, Daniel and I both orbited around Zev and were anchored by his sunny, happy nature. The little round-cheeked blond boy that inhabited our hearts seemed to skip through life with little misery. There were scrapes and disappointments, but it didn't take much to hit the default switch and find the smiles and the giggles. He wanted to hold on to his happiness the way some hold on to their unhappiness.

My illness had been a presence in our lives almost from his birth, so he didn't know anything different. He experienced my illness as if it were another hair colour or a particular contour of nose. There was no reason for him to worry.

But surely what delighted and distracted us most from our problems was the way in which Zev expressed his excitement and creativity. He approached life with open arms and an open mouth, ready to embrace the next adventure. From an early age, Zev had developed intense passions. There had been the red phase, where he would wear nothing but red from head to toe. There was a brief zebra phase that involved white clothes and black electrician's tape. And he once spent an entire week in the heat of the Caribbean wearing a nylon Batman costume, getting smellier and stickier by the day. The resort staff were delighted to greet him with, "Hola, Batman!" and he would return their greetings and flex his muscles.

The most enduring and endearing passion, however, was the bagpipe phase. Zev's fire for bagpipes was fuelled by a

Canada Day parade in Stratford. He was mesmerized by the three bagpipe bands that marched past us and after the parade, studied the pictures that we had taken. His daycare teacher, bless her heart, picked up on Zev's fascination and made him a CD of bagpipe music. I remember the way the CD saved us on a six-hour drive with three-year-old Zev. The minute it stopped, we would hear a whimper from the back and would restart the music.

Daniel and I developed a nighttime routine for Zev. When it was time to go to bed, we would pretend to have bagpipes and, with a nasal dirge-like sound, do our vocal rendition of "Scotland the Brave." Zev would march, and we would march, and all this marching would steer us up the stairs and into Zev's bedroom. This became so ingrained in our evening ritual that he might be crying about leaving his activity, but when we started to drone, his legs would start marching of their own accord and he would march upstairs through his tears. We were shameless in our use of it.

I went to the Goodwill and found a tartan skirt that could act as a kilt. Zev wore that kilt (or its replacement) almost every day for about two years. He wore it over his pants in the cold weather and barelegged the rest of the time. His favourite combination was wearing the kilt with his Super-man Underoos, the blue Superman shirt on top, the kilt below. And, if you asked, he would pull up the kilt to reveal the red underwear underneath. That outfit was his happy place. And that made it our happy place.

We were lucky. We got the child we needed; a happy, healthy, easy-going child. We knew how lucky we were. We worked hard to protect him from the storm that my illness created, wanting to provide a safe harbour. But as I reflect back, it was perhaps he who provided the safe harbour for us.

28

M Y HEMATOLOGIST WAS leaving to work in the
United States and distributed his patients among
the other doctors in the clinic.

"I'm giving you to Dr. Reece. You'll like her. She's more
touchy-feely." His little smile told me what he thought about
touchy-feely and, perhaps, what he thought about me.

It turns out that touchy-feely meant things like looking at
me, asking me questions to which she wanted the answers
and engaging with me as a partner in my own care. Every visit
she would print out my blood work results and we would pore
over them together. She would point out the significant numbers and teach me how to navigate the complicated pages.

Her skill in interacting with her patients was matched
by her intelligence and drive. She was fiercely smart and
seemed to have an encyclopedic memory. If I asked her a
question, no matter how silly, I would watch her flip through
her mental Rolodex and pluck out all necessary facts and
studies to offer a thoughtful, complete and respectful answer.
She was a leader in both the amyloid and multiple myeloma
communities and fought like a mother bear for her patients.
From the first appointment, I knew I'd hit the jackpot.

I had come to assume that the behaviour of my first doctor was the norm; that I would always feel like a little kid,

feet dangling, under the gaze of the big, important doctor. He would be communicative and charming with my doctor sisters but would rarely engage me in discussion. Dr. Reece assumed I wanted to fully engage, and each appointment was a full review of what was happening with my health as if I was a thinking adult.

—

DR. REECE TOLD me that the thalidomide, which had become so beloved to me, was no longer working. It took me a while to understand her. Once a drug worked, it kept working forever, didn't it? Thalidomide was my wonder drug.

I was thrown for a loop. I learned then that a medication would work for a while, until it didn't. Every medication had an expiry date... a mystery expiry date. Why had nobody explained that important concept before? Or maybe they had, and I hadn't heard it. With that understanding, there was no relaxing into a routine with a medication. Surely, we would eventually run out of medications.

From my first doctor I had learned that there was no true cure for my illness, it was only controlled as long as a drug was working. And now from my second doctor I learned that any drug could stop working at any moment.

It was hard not to throw up my hands and give up. I'm far too good at playing out worst-case scenarios and it takes courage to live with the knowledge that things could go south at any moment. I was tempted to close myself in and eat bonbons all day. But my doctor was encouraging, telling me that there were many medications that might work for me and that the first new one we were going to try looked promising.

—

WITH THALIDOMIDE OFF the table, the next drug in line was a new kind of smart drug called Velcade. I had visions of little molecules of drugs carrying clipboards, using pocket protectors and wearing glasses held together with duct tape. Or better yet, trained killers who could move stealthily through the body, only knocking off those cells on their hit list. Unlike chemo, which was more like mass murder, smart drugs were focused in their tasks. Go, my little hit men, and take no prisoners.

The only problem with this medication was that I had to go once a week to the Princess Margaret Hospital chemo unit in Toronto, two to three hours from my home in Stratford. Once again, just as we had settled into a routine, we had to recalibrate our lives to accommodate this new change. Of course, anything can become normal with time.

Those little hit men knew their stuff. Velcade was a wonder drug. It had fewer side effects than any other drug I had been on. I felt healthier than I had in a long time. The time that I was on Velcade was like a renaissance for me. I had more energy for my family and energy to help with cooking and cleaning. I took over the bookkeeping for Daniel's business and became more deeply involved with administration and teaching with Taoist Tai Chi. I increased my commitment to our synagogue by teaching religious school, leading services, joining the board. Later, I began a master of fine arts in creative writing through the University of British Columbia. It was "optional residency," so I could do it part-time from a distance. I even did a bit of paid work.

I still had rough days and sometimes rough months, like when nobody noticed that the iron levels in my blood had hit rock bottom for several months, causing an unrelenting fatigue. Still, I felt like I could take on more than I had in years. It seemed we were moving back toward our imagined future instead of away from it.

This was a shiny time in our family. Zev was older and the work of caring for him was less intense. He was more independent and increasingly more interesting and more lovely. I had a greater store of energy that allowed me to be with him and actually do something more active than read a book. When I could, I brought him with me to the tai chi centre and he became a familiar presence there.

I enjoyed being able to help Daniel at work and at home, decreasing his burden. I was still experiencing such guilt about my earlier absences that I felt I should pour all my newfound energy into our common cause. This didn't always serve me well. My energy was better, but it was still limited. So, I would swing one way—working hard on house and business, doing less tai chi—and would become tired and stiff. Then I would go do more tai chi and the tension between us would return.

But I was feeling back in the current of the world. While it was stressful at times with all I had taken on, I felt like my identity was restored. I wasn't a parasite. I was a busy woman with purpose. As we always did, we assumed, unconsciously, that we would go on like this forever.

29

WITH THE ADDITION of the fifty-two visits a year to Princess Margaret Hospital for delivery of Velcade, I was now racking up almost one hundred medical visits a year. Between wait time and appointment time, my total time in medical facilities every year was almost three hundred hours. Or about six hours per week, not including travel time. A part-time job.

Over half of those hours were spent in the waiting room, so I became a waiting-room veteran, an expert. Call me the waiting-room maven. If Michelin were to do a guide to hospital waiting rooms in Toronto and environs, I could be their agent on the ground.

I'm not looking for sympathy; I simply want to establish my credentials in this matter. I know the squishy farting noise that the ubiquitous vinyl-covered chairs make as people shift in their seats. I know that the televisions will be forever tuned to the local sensational news station (except for the one blood clinic where they play *I Love Lucy* reruns). I know that the more modern variety of waiting rooms will be decorated in dusty rose, blue or beige, so much so that I crave vivid, dangerous colours after a day spent in these sanitary, pastel paradises.

Escaping from the hospital and grabbing a few minutes to write during a long appointment. Notice the hospital bracelet on my arm.

I can provide you with the insider details that a casual visitor would miss. For example, the plushest waiting area and cleanest washrooms are in the breast clinic at Mount Sinai Hospital. I've noticed that the receptionist at the Princess Margaret Hospital chemo unit, who appears to be in a bad mood, is kind and funny, in that slow, sardonic way, when you get to know her. It helps if you bring chocolate at Christmas. Someone at the kidney clinic at Toronto General Hospital likes to post signs such as *Please put your garbage in the can and not on the floor*. I have been tempted to post one that reads *Please pee into the toilet and not into the sink*.

I understand the way people shift around in waiting spaces, elevators and lineups like salt molecules in a beaker of water, claiming their full territory within the given parameters. The movements to equidistance are unconscious.

I can spot the good waiters, those who calmly observe the world around them. Like the lean, aging cowboy who click-clacked into a waiting room one day with his cane and sharp boots, a long grey ponytail snaking out from under his cowboy hat. He looked absolutely at ease, as if there were nowhere else he'd rather be.

And I've witnessed those whose struggles to wait have resulted in tantrums. Like the woman in narrow rectangular glasses that made her eyes look small and beady, like little bugs. Her face appeared to be only bug eyes and a big angry mouth while she yelled over and over again to the poor receptionist, "I've been coming here ten years and I've never had to wait this long before," as the rest of us in the waiting room stared, happily horrified by this outrageous behaviour.

I tried not to bring anyone with me to my appointments. After years of cultivating my waiting-room stamina, I could be patient with the longest wait times, the dingiest waiting rooms or the most inefficient clinic managers. I could do the long haul. But when I brought others, they would fidget and sigh in exasperation. "How can you stand it?"

———

VELCADE WAS A mild, non-chemo drug that took less than a minute to administer, but each week I faced a mountain of a wait before I even made it to a chair. It was an opportunity for some serious wait training.

When I first started, I saw waiting as a black hole of time. The world was going on without me, while I was trapped like a mandarin orange in a Jell-O mould. I had no control, I could only wait there, helpless, until it was my turn to be plucked out of the waiting room and sent in for my treatment. My real, vibrant and important life was held hostage to the time in this inefficient jail and would only begin moving again once the waiting was over. I ranted to anyone who would listen about the soul-sucking nature of waiting rooms.

Flipping through an abandoned newspaper one day in my usual chair in the atrium, I spotted a picture with a long line of people waiting. I zeroed in on the caption. The people were lined up for food in a relief camp in Pakistan. Most of them looked at ease with their bodies and at ease with the wait, despite the fact that they were waiting for life-giving food.

With that picture in mind, my radar was set to spot other images of waiting people. Women queuing up in long lines for water in the Central African Republic; long lines of voters clutching their ballots in rural India. And in every picture, I saw patience and calm in the faces and bodies of the waiting people.

I reflected on my own frustrations with waiting. It occurred to me that in the West, we feel that we have a right to be protected from waiting. We "tsk, tsk" the customer service in an establishment if we have to wait more than a nanosecond to be served. We demand our proper turn. We get snippy with service staff. We devote an entire academic discipline, queuing theory, to exploring how mathematical models might reduce our wait times, or at least distract us from them, like children.

My impatience implied that my time was too important to be spent on this mundane act of waiting. But was it? Perhaps if I were in the midst of developing a life-saving vaccine or negotiating the end of hostilities in the Middle East I could say that. In truth, I wanted a quick escape out of that hospital because I was restless and bored.

Maybe where I saw a black hole, other people, other cultures, saw an opportunity for quiet, stillness and a readiness to engage with the world. Perhaps if I were to view waiting as my occupation rather than as something to endure, I might resist it less.

—

ONE TUESDAY BEFORE my appointment with my doctor, I poked my head into the waiting room of the blood lab at Princess Margaret. I felt as if I been transported to a crowded market bazaar. Nurses and volunteers called names and numbers like street hawkers. There was a steady buzz of conversation in at least four languages. Patients and their loved ones were squeezed into every available seat, juggling coats, bags and coffee cups. The ones left standing leaned against walls and poles and looked longingly at the chairs or milled about in the lobby. The long registration line, in its cramped space, was scattered every so often by a speeding wheelchair, only to form again in the chair's wake.

In the early days of being sick, I would have sighed at my lot in having to spend so much time in this crowded waiting room. But my views on waiting had evolved and I was more willing to engage in and reflect upon what I found there.

I looked around at the other patients. The beautiful girl with the long black hair, sitting holding her head in hands while her—sister? friend? lover?—sat beside her rubbing her back. The older couple, leaning into each other and working on a crossword. The woman in a business suit, clutching her coat as if it were a lifesaving float. Where would all these people be if they weren't here? Surely every one of them had sat in a doctor's office hearing some version of, "I have the results," and been thrown off whatever life trajectory they had been following.

Each of them would have their own individual tales of waiting, but there was no doubt that waiting was a central part of their illness experience. I considered the many different types of waiting I had faced since getting sick. There were, of course, the hours and hours in the waiting rooms. That was like fingernails on a chalkboard or Muzak: annoying, but not all that serious. But what about the tense weeks filled with waiting for the diagnosis? That was like hearing the siren of a fire truck or an ambulance approaching and not knowing if it was going to stop at your house or keep going. The wait for my stem-cell transplant was like the sound of the fire alarm in a tall building, the panic, not knowing where the fire was, feeling the need to act, imagining the worst.

After I survived the treatment, I had to wait for recovery, wait for hair, wait for my taste buds, wait for energy to return. That was a slow dirge on an out-of-tune organ. It was easy to believe that this music would carry on forever.

The most painful yearning, however, accompanied the wait to get back to the life I had planned; to get back to what I thought was my *real* life.

This waiting came to a head one Sunday afternoon as I was cleaning my closet. I was purging, and the garbage bag of give-away clothes was filling up as I culled down to the essentials. I wanted more space and less stuff. Everything had to be tried on and I was ruthless.

"Doesn't fit." Into the bag.

"Colour is terrible!" Into the bag.

"Mutton dressed as lamb!" Into the bag.

And then, as I worked my way to the back of the cupboard, I spotted my suit, my one beautiful, slim, iron-grey suit. The one my mother had bought me. I saw it and my determination flagged.

I pulled it out of the cupboard and sat down on the bed, clutching it to me. I didn't need to try it on, I knew I was long past fitting into it. The belly now made wearing the suit impossible.

I had worn that suit to every important meeting and conference, feeling sharp and confident. I had been back in action and I had been hot, making new contacts, soliciting new contracts, growing my career. That suit felt like my lucky outfit, to be worn when I wanted to feel talented and successful.

When the crushing fatigue had returned a year after the transplant and it was clear that I needed to give up my contracts and refocus on my health, I had exchanged the suit for my rubber ducky flannel pajamas and my world had shrunk to the dimensions of my bedroom. Once again, my life was suspended, and I lay in bed, adjusting to new medication, awaiting my second coming. I kept the suit, believing it would not be long before I was up and about and back at work.

As the years passed, the possibility of going back to work seemed increasingly remote. My energy waxed and waned and could not be counted upon. I still waited. I still kept the suit. Even though my time away from work became greater than the time I had spent working, even though the suit no longer fit. I would stroke it every so often, saying to myself, "When I am better, I will need that suit."

Back in my bedroom, surrounded by discarded clothes, I sat holding the suit, rocking myself, remembering the person I had been before, that person who had energy, who could get up for work in the morning and drive places and work a conference. Who was I fooling by keeping this suit? I was no longer that person and I didn't know if I ever would be again. There was no point in waiting any longer. This life that I had, this life of illness, *this* was my life.

I sat until daylight disappeared and I was in darkness. The sound that accompanied my revelations was the "Lacrymosa" from Mozart's *Requiem*. It is a tune of grieving, full of keening pain. This music accompanied me in my mind through this grief, rising and falling until it finally resolved with the plea for eternal rest for the dead and a thundering "AMEN."

I could hear my family downstairs making dinner. I folded the suit and put it in the bag, trying not to cry. In the cupboard there was a yawning pit where the suit had been. It threatened to pull me into its darkness. I pulled a string of other clothes over to fill the space and closed the door. "Amen."

—

AFTER GIVING UP the suit, a blackness opened up in my world. This wait to return to what I thought was a normal life had infused every part of me, it was the filter through which I had viewed the world. I lay in my bed for days, staring at the trees outside my window, believing that without that "real" life to look forward to, there wasn't much point in anything.

30

"COURAGE LIVES HERE" was spray-painted on the sidewalk in front of the hospital. I stopped to stare at this statement as the flow of harried commuters grumbled around me. The words put me on edge right away, but I couldn't find the source of this irritation. These kinds of rousing declarations were seen all over the place, in ads or on T-shirts at fundraising events. I knew the words were meant to inspire, but my first thought was that it would be more appropriate to say, "Pain, shit, blood and vomit live here, yet we persist. *That* is courage."

I resumed my walk to the subway, but the words stayed with me. How did most people feel upon entering the hospital? Would this statement make them feel more courageous or would it make them feel that they weren't living up to expectations? There was enough pressure on patients to "fight" and "have hope." I had felt the pressure to be the perfect mother and now I was increasingly feeling the pressure to be the perfect patient. It could be called "patienting" and it had its own culture of wheatgrass juice and positive thinking. I'd been told by one person that my illness was a result of my anger management problem. Another told me it was unresolved grief for my father. A friend with an aggressive, fatal cancer was told by other friends that if she took the chemo, which could save her life, she was taking poison into her body.

I do have some understanding of this perspective. "Why isn't anyone paying attention to what Daddy's eating?" I harassed my sisters with this, believing that perhaps if he ate more tofu, he would be saved from his aggressive leukemia. I was young and had no idea. I had no idea what it was like to have your taste buds skewed, so you're happy to get any food down at all. I had no idea of how important a role food could play in brightening a heavily medical day. I had no idea that when you know you're dying, you're not so interested in watching your cholesterol.

I had to bite my tongue when I heard people talk about survivors as "real fighters," implying that those who didn't survive, weren't fighters or weren't courageous enough. A culture of blame and judgement toward patients was growing, evoking feelings of guilt among those already struggling with the emotional trauma of deep illness. If you weren't doing all of the right things, then you held some responsibility in your illness.

"So, what would you say?" Daniel asked, tired of my ranting.

Each of us experiences courage in a unique and personal manner. For me it's a deep river inside from which I draw thimblefuls at a time. Sometimes it dries up while other times it gushes. Sometimes the courage is for facing the monsters, like my stem-cell transplant. Other times it's for carrying on after a day full of little problems that alone would have been innocuous, but collectively were overwhelming.

It's easy to label someone as courageous or an "inspiration," but most of us are just doing what we have to do. Isn't that what everyone is doing all the time in life? And what choice do we have? For me, I needed the most courage when I felt trapped in the relentlessness of my illness. No matter how much I stamped my feet, I still needed to get out of my pajamas, take my pills, submit to medical tests and go to my doctors' appointments. And I had to do all of that knowing I would have to do it the next day and the day after that. And knowing that it would never get any better, only worse.

When I woke Daniel at night to sob and tell him that I couldn't do this anymore, I didn't want to be given a Hallmark card for my courage. Trite words and slogans didn't help me in any way except to make me feel patronized.

So, what would I say?

As a patient who, like all patients, did not choose a life of illness, I needed empathy and support, not pity. My ideal slogan? Words which would give me courage? "This is hard, and we are here to help."

31

TIME PASSED, PUNCTUATED by moments of crisis and long stretches of just living. Zev grew and grew and grew when we weren't looking. Before we knew it, we were preparing for his bar mitzvah.

Zev looked magnificent up on the *bima*[1] in his pink shirt, striped tie and formal black pants. He was cloaked in his brand new *tallit*[2] decorated for him in honour of his bar mitzvah by our magical artist friend, Mary. She had sewn on a whimsical climbing vine using material taken from bits and pieces of our lives. There was even one of the birds from our wedding canopy, transformed into two dimensions, sitting on the vine.

Our normally slouchy thirteen-year-old stood tall and looked out at his audience with a confidence I had never had at that age. His Torah reading had unfolded well; he had spoken the Hebrew words, words he had had to learn from scratch, without a mistake. Now he was giving his commentary on the Torah portion.

---

1   Altar in a synagogue
2   Prayer shawl

Zev with his proud and happy parents on the *bima* at his bar mitzvah

Those are the two central pieces of the ceremony. When a boy or girl turns thirteen, they become *bar* or *bat mitzvah* and are then considered adults in the eyes of the Jewish community. As only adults are permitted to read from the Torah, the ceremony is focused around that very first reading. Then, in the Jewish tradition of analysis and debate, the bar or bat mitzvah delivers a commentary that provides the congregation with a new way of looking at the reading or raises questions about it to consider.

Zev had decided to read the very first portion of the Torah for his ceremony, the story of creation. "Let there be light..." With his commentary, he managed, in seven minutes, to reconcile the age-old debate of religion versus science, even sliding in a quote from Albert Einstein. The synagogue was full of our family, friends and fellow congregants, who were all smiles. They had come from all over Canada and the United States. They were there for Zev. They were there for us and for our parents. That can be the nature of these events; the gathering of the clans. The chance to come together and say, "We are a family and we are here for you." Daniel and I had put heart and soul into making this a meaningful experience for Zev. He looked as radiant as a thirteen-year-old boy could look. We told him to take the time to scan the room and record in his head all of the people who loved him and would be there for him if he ever needed them. Even if he wouldn't remember this moment, for me it was a great comfort to see the big net of caring people that had Zev's back.

There was a moment in the service when the grandparents and we, the parents, stood in a row to symbolically hand Zev the Torah down through the generations. There was my mother, Roberta, and Daniel's parents, Barbara and Leon.

Zev had (and still has) three living grandparents, which for me, having only grown up with one, felt very rich. I ached, though, for my father's absence. He would have adored Zev. He would have adored all his grandchildren.

The rabbi beamed as she came up to say a few words at the end; the affection between her and Zev was clear. She asked Zev some unplanned questions about his commentary and he answered without any hesitation. An old hand.

I could breathe a sigh of relief. I had hoped to live to see Zev's bar mitzvah ceremony; to know that at least in the eyes of the Jewish people, he had made it to adulthood. Everything from then on would be gravy.

At least that was what I had said to myself. In reality I was holding on by every fingernail wanting to be with him for as long as I could. I was grateful to have lived this long, but it would not have been enough to only live until his bar mitzvah. I was hungry to watch him develop through those adolescent years, to find his passion, perhaps to meet the love of his life. I was not ready. Would I ever be? It was hard to imagine.

32

ZEV'S BAR MITZVAH had been in the fall of 2012. Less than a year later, the Velcade stopped working. It had been my favourite treatment to date. I had had more energy on Velcade than on any treatment before. Life was busy but it was wonderful to be able to "pull my weight" in the world, to feel useful. Now my little hit men had stopped taking orders.

My doctor had the next drug ready. It was a derivative of thalidomide. Thalidomide had been good for me, so I started this new drug confident that it would work as well as the others.

Except it didn't. Not only did it not work, but it took my kidneys down with it. They had been getting worse, but very slowly. Over the few months that I took this medication, my kidneys took a sharp decline. While it clearly worked for many people, this one was not my friend.

It was at this moment that my doctor told me she had nothing else for me. With the decline in kidney function, I was no longer eligible for the next drug she would have normally tried. All she could do was offer supportive care to the end.

I was still feeling well from having been on Velcade, so the idea of dying felt theoretical. Yet, according to my doctor, it was real. This was the moment when I made pickles, when I knit blankets, when I retreated to the tai chi centre. My doctor had never spoken to me with such grave foreboding before. She had never used the word *dire*.

—

I HAD FELT strong enough while I was on Velcade that I had been able to be active, part of the world. Almost normal, with something that felt like purpose.

When things became dire, though, I gave up every one of my responsibilities. My energy was waning and I felt the need to focus on my health without other distractions. I retreated to the tai chi centre again and practiced as much as I could. I tried to contain the worry about my abstract death.

My days became hazy, merging into one another. I felt I had no purpose, no identity. I was a parasite sitting around waiting to die. Without the usual markers of worth, I felt of little value. If I was with new people and they asked me what I "did," I had no idea what to say. I had stripped right down to the bone, and all that was left was me. I wasn't sure if that was enough.

—

IT WAS DURING this time that visions of my father started to enter my mind.

"My three *maziks!*" my father would exclaim over his beloved young daughters before suffocating us with hugs and wet kisses. He was unable to contain his joy over the magnificence of our *mazikness* and his luck in having three daughters to whom he could bestow his affection. This Yiddish term of endearment, we were told, meant something like "little mouse," although when I researched the meaning recently, I saw that it meant "rascal" or "imp."

"You're such a mazik," he said to me when I displayed great prescience or told a good joke or, sometimes, when I was doing nothing at all. Often there were hugs and kisses, sometimes a face squeezed between excited hands.

This expression of love never wavered as we became teenagers.

"You're such a mazik!" my father kissed me with his stubbly face as I tried to swallow Tylenol for my menstrual cramps without gagging or choking.

"Da-ad," I said in two-syllable exasperation. "I'm in the middle of something!"

While explaining the deep significance of the Stanislavski method I'd learned about in my drama class, my father shook his head in amazement and interrupted my monologue to say, "You're such a mazik!"

"Uh, yeah, Dad, anyway, what I was saying..."

With the assurance only a teenager could hold, I dismissed my father's pronouncement. I was certain that my father didn't "get" the real me. I knew what I was and what I wasn't. He knew a kewpie doll version of me. He would pat me on the head, label me a *mazik* and send me off to my mother for the harder stuff. The word *mazik* seemed invented by him, I never heard it anywhere else, and I came to associate it with a burden.

I moved away for university, setting out to shape my identity around my ideals of intellect, morals and aesthetics. I wanted to be cool. I wanted to be sharp. I wanted to change the world. I left my mazikness with my stuffed animals and only picked it up with reluctance on my visits home.

There is a scene that repeated itself over and over again in my late teens and early twenties. I would be in my room in whatever shared house I had arranged, in whatever city I happened to be studying in that year, surrounded by milk-crate bookcases, art posters and an Ikea desk. I would be weeping and hugging my knees, gasping great sobs and shaking.

"Why aren't I a different person?" I would ask myself over and over. Why wasn't I smarter, prettier, deeper, more curious, more interesting? When I would add up my dismal attributes, they did not amount to anything lovable or useful in the world. I can't think of my youth without remembering the despair of these self-assessments.

When my father died, I was ready to let the term *mazik* die with him. I wanted to stamp my foot and declare myself to be far deeper and more complex than the word *mazik* could convey. But, when Zev was born, it was necessary to thaw my dislike of the word, because he was so clearly a mazik. A little chubby-cheeked package of perfection. It seemed the only word that could properly contain the massive love I was feeling for him.

I supposed that had my father been around when I could not find myself, he would have been calling me a mazik, whether I was working or not, healthy or sick, fatigued or engaged. At that moment of feeling useless, I found comfort in the idea that I could still be a mazik.

I thought then about the love I had for my husband and son, for my family, for my friends. I didn't love Daniel because I made a list of the good and the bad things about him. I didn't love him because he had a job or was useful in some capacity. I loved him for his Danielness. The whole of him, the spirit of him that shone through. I could get pissed off at him, but I never lost my love for that kindly spirit. I likewise loved Zev for his Zevness. And perhaps it was because I loved his Zevness that I loved his sense of humour, his view of the world, and his other attributes.

So when I stripped away my markers of identity, I didn't have to strip away my mazikness. It was the core of my spirit. My Samness would always be with me and those people who valued my Samness would continue to do so, even if I was missing these other more superficial markers.

I don't think my dad necessarily thought this all through; it was a default setting. He was the type of man that could love someone in their wholeness, without judgment or expectation. It wasn't until twenty years after his death that I finally got him. And I got him when I most needed him.

33

AT DINNER ONE night a few years ago, I asked, "Zev, was it hard for you when I was away so much?"

"I like the way you and Papa gave me so much independence. It was different. If you were away, it was Papa and me time. If you were home, we had time together and that was good. I like being on my own." Our sixteen-year-old son went on to recall the time that Daniel bought him a can of spray whipped cream when I was away and let him spray it right into his mouth. A childhood dream come true; it never would have happened had I been home. Then he turned back to his food, which was of far more interest to him than this conversation. I let him eat while I considered.

Memories of my own childhood came to mind. When I was ten my mother had returned to work and my greatest memory is the joy I felt during the hour at lunch and the first hour after school when I was completely alone. I didn't have to answer to anyone. That sweet taste of freedom helped me to cultivate independence and confidence in myself to be alone. I would have hated having my mother around all the time hovering over me.

So, my absences were not harmful. I still wanted to understand, however, if I was a good mother. Was my illness traumatic for Zev? Did all of my absences and my lack of close attention have dire consequences for my child?

I peered at Zev as he inhaled his dinner. He loomed over me from a height of six foot two with size-twelve feet, a gold-stud earring and his long hair in a bun. When we were out together, Zev would engage with other adults, asking thoughtful questions. He looked after his friends when they were in need. He was able to experience joy from a beautiful meal, a good canoe ride, an awesome video game. He was still a teenager in countless ways, such as his youthful impatience towards the obtuseness of his parents, but his teenageness was mild and he was already so much the man he would become. Zev was very much his own person. Daniel and I gave him the space to be who he was and loved him like crazy.

Like me, he seemed to thrive on independence and grow stronger because of it. Unlike me, he did not doubt himself. Maybe I wasn't the perfect mother, but he didn't appear to care. I could still wrap myself in a knot if I started ticking off in my head all the field trips I didn't attend and the birthday cakes I didn't bake. But here was Zev telling me and clearly demonstrating that all was fine. Who should I have been listening to? The imaginary voices in my head or my real-life, flesh-and-blood son?

I may not have been the perfect mother, but in the end, it would seem that through no intention of my own, I got enough out of the way to be the mother Zev needed me to be. Hallelujah.

PART SEVEN

14.   15.

34

IMAGINE BIG RED flashing lights here and a sign that reads:

BEWARE!
DIALYSIS AHEAD.
POINT OF NO RETURN!

Kidneys are nothing short of miraculous. Everyone makes a big deal about the heart and the lungs, but without those kidneys working away in the background, life would be impossible. They help regulate blood pressure and red blood cell production and support bone development. They remove excess fluid and filter excess minerals and toxins out of the blood. They not only take out what's not needed, they *know* what's not needed. They read the body and perceive that you are holding too much potassium and remove the excess. They recognize outside toxins and filter those out. They know you're dehydrated after your day at the beach and don't produce as much urine.

Blood enters your kidneys "dirty" and exits scrubbed clean and fluid balanced. Every day the kidneys perform their magic on your blood over and over again. They don't sleep or take vacations. Smart and dedicated to boot, these are organs to celebrate.

My kidneys began their decline in secret. For years we hardly thought about them and focused on my liver and lymph nodes. At the time there appeared to be no amyloid deposits in the kidneys.

The blood marker called creatinine is one of the ways to track kidney function. Creatinine is a waste product that normal kidneys will eliminate. When levels of creatinine began to rise in my blood a few years into my illness, we decided I should start seeing a nephrologist.

My sister, Shelley, is a nephrologist, a kidney doctor. But she could not be *my* kidney doctor because it would have been a conflict of interest, her being my sister and all. Doctors, as a rule, do not treat their own kin, although both of my sisters have been intimately involved with my care from the beginning.

I was assigned to an excellent Toronto nephrologist, who I saw for a yearly chat and check-in. We would agree that my kidneys were doing well. He would add *for now*, and then ask me to come back in a year. I would stand up to leave and shrug on my coat, my mind already thinking ahead to my drive home to Stratford. At that moment, my doctor would drop a stealth bomb at my feet.

"One of these days, Sam, we'll have to start talking about a kidney transplant [*Kaboom!!*] but not today." He would smile. "See you next time. Say 'Hi' to your sister."

or

"One of these days we'll probably be looking at dialysis [*Kaboom!!*], but we can talk about that another time." He would smile. "Talk to my secretary on your way out about your next appointment."

Kidney transplant? Dialysis? These were far-off and unknown and he dropped them into my life with no warning and no explanation. The bombs exploded into a million fragments of worry that embedded themselves into my flesh.

—

EVENTUALLY, MY CREATININE and other marker tests were high enough that we explored my options with more depth and less stealth. By the end of 2012, we had ruled out the possibility of a kidney transplant because of my underlying illness and had set our sights on dialysis. I was transferred to a nephrologist in my catchment area who would look after my transition into dialysis. He worked out of London, Ontario, only an hour from my home in Stratford.

My new nephrologist was a wry Scottish man with a strong brogue who earned my devotion and respect from the first meeting.

"Sam, I'm not going to rush you into dialysis. I don't care what the bloody numbers say; it's about how you feel. I trust that you're sensible enough not to suffer in silence. We'll take this nice and slow." I wanted to kiss his feet.

—

IT USED TO be that if your kidneys stopped working you died. But modern times have given us the ingenious dialysis machine. Dialysis recreates the actions of the kidney outside of the body. When I dialyze, one tube carries the "dirty" blood out of my body and into the pretend kidney (the dialyzer). Another tube carries the improved blood back into my body. Bye-bye, potassium. Bye-bye, toxins. Hoses that attach to the dialyzer can remove excess fluid. Bye-bye, swollen feet.

I travelled to see my nephrologist every three months and we watched the blood work with close attention. One day at an appointment, he lingered over the blood test results. Then he sighed and turned to me.

"Okay, Sam. Your creatine is quite high, but I still feel that you'll know best when you're ready for dialysis. What I'm worried about is you having some kind of emergency and needing dialysis all of sudden." He tapped his pen on his desk as he thought. "So, I'll make you a deal." He thumped the desk as he said this. "How about you have the surgery to create your fistula and then you can wait as long as you want, knowing that you're ready for any emergency?"

Another reprieve.

———

I WORKED WITH an exceptionally kind and skilled surgeon at St. Michael's Hospital in Toronto (and as a bonus I could add St. Mike's to my hospital life-list). The surgeon created a fistula by joining a vein and an artery to make a vessel that could accommodate the extra blood flow generated by dialysis. I have a fistula that pops out of my upper left arm as if it were a highly developed muscle—almost cartoonish, like Popeye. It's not exactly attractive, but it looks as if I've been eating my spinach.

At first, I covered it up in embarrassment. Aside from its size, it was a little rough-looking from the bruising that I had in the early days of needling. One summer, with temperatures leaping up above thirty-four degrees Celsius, I lost my shyness about it. People didn't ask about the fistula the way they asked if I was pregnant; instead, they stared.

One day at Staples my cashier, an awkward high-school student, extolled the virtue of the top-up warrantee for the new hard drive I was purchasing. "No, no, no, I don't want it." I shook my head and waved my hands, indicating for him to stop. Several times. But it didn't matter what I said, he wasn't speaking to me. He was explaining the policy to my fistula, who put up no protest at all.

The flow of blood in the fistula was so tremendous that I could hear it at night; a *whoosh whoosh* sound, almost like the ocean. When you touched the fistula it felt alive and a little creepy. That feeling is called "the thrill" and I was to ensure that I could always "feel my thrill." My thrill was never in doubt; my fistula was powerful. The first time the nurse inserted the needle to hook me up to the dialysis machine, the epic force of the fistula sent out a spray of blood that showered us all.

35

OR SOME MYSTERIOUS reason, my creatinine dropped after the fistula surgery. "It happens sometimes," Shelley said. This meant we didn't need to jump into dialysis right away. I knew that many activities would, ultimately, be curtailed once I started dialysis. My life would centre around my medical schedule, leaving me only tiny pockets of time and energy to get away. Thus, I wanted to take advantage of any non-dialysis time left to do the activities that were important to me.

I attended endless tai chi classes and week-long tai chi retreats. I attended a two-week residency at the University of British Columbia in Vancouver as part of my MFA degree in creative writing. Daniel and I took a five-day driving vacation. My entire family travelled to Montreal to celebrate my mother's eightieth birthday. None of it was exotic or France, but it felt like bonus time. This free run lasted about a year before things changed.

Into the second year, my creatinine started rising again. Then, for the first time, I started to experience new, unpleasant sensations. Sometimes my hands would cramp up into claws. It would feel like curved iron bars had penetrated my hands and taken them hostage. My hands were helpless to resist, shot full of pain until the moment passed and the muscles could release. Sometimes, at night, it would be needles in my shins or flaming rods in my thighs.

I experienced bouts of extreme fatigue. One day I called Daniel from the car in the driveway. Through my tears I asked him to come home because I didn't have the energy to get from the car to the house.

On top of the cramping and fatigue, my taste buds started to let me down. Food wasn't tasting right, and I went from one disappointing meal to another. I lost weight I couldn't afford to lose. Once my kidney problems started messing with my food, I knew it was time. Shelley kept encouraging me, letting me know that I would feel much better once I was on dialysis. It had taken years for me to give in. Finally, the symptoms were less tolerable than the idea of dialysis.

—

DANIEL AND I sat in the kidney clinic office.

"So," my Scottish nephrologist said, looking over my blood work. "How are you today?" He turned away from the computer and looked directly at me, as if he really wanted to know. It still seemed like a novel experience to me.

"I think I'm ready to start dialysis. I'm not totally sure..." I was half hoping that he would say, "Nah, Sam, let's wait a while longer." Instead, he gave me no room to back out. He jumped up and called in one of the nurses who trained dialysis patients.

"Sam is ready to start her dialysis training."

The nurse looked at me and smiled. "That's great news, Sam! Well, you and I will be spending a lot of time together. Let's look at this calendar." We picked a starting date and ran through the schedule. She left us and we were alone again with the doctor.

"Well, I'm glad you're starting, Sam. Your creatinine was starting to make me nervous."

This was news to me. He'd always seemed cool with my desire to push for my freedom as long as possible. But maybe I had waited longer than he had expected. If he had been worried, he had hidden it well behind a poker face.

—

"GOOD FOR YOU for making that hard decision!" wrote my friend Susan, from New Zealand. Up until that moment, every time I had told someone that I was starting dialysis, the conversation would usually end in tears and hugs and comforting noises. Most people responded the way I would have responded: "I'm so sorry." "Oh, that's going to be so tough." And I would get wobbly and try to rein in the tears, which had become a habit.

One of my tai chi instructors told me to stop resisting something I had no choice about. "If the sky is cloudy, wrap yourself in it as a blanket," was the poetry he brought out to help ease my worry. Then I received Susan's note, which made me sit up a little straighter. "Yes, good for me." Maybe I didn't need to cry anymore. Maybe I was a strong woman, tackling my health issues with courage. I didn't totally believe it, but at least I stopped the crying.

36

THE TWO TECH guys took command as soon as they entered our house.

"Let's start with the room where you want to dialyze," one said. The other one held up his hands and gave us each a meaningful look.

"I'm a tough guy when it comes to safety and keeping the equipment properly maintained," he warned us.

He looked more teddy bear than tough guy. His puppy dog eyes exuded kindness and his speech was a mellow music. We nodded in obedience and then led them to our bedroom.

I had chosen to do home dialysis rather than go to a clinic. Getting a dialysis machine at home was a big deal. It's not like owning a vacuum, where you plug it in, turn it on and then put it in the closet when you're done. The machine is expensive and has needs. We would also need a reverse osmosis (RO) water-filter machine and a new water softener. The government would pay for all the equipment I needed, all of the supplies required on a monthly basis, as well as training and support from a team of fabulous nurses, and even an electricity rebate for the additional electricity used by the machines.

In the long run, it was cheaper for the government to put all of this equipment in our home than to have me dialyze in a clinic. Of course, it had benefits for me as well. Patients who did home dialysis often had better outcomes than those that didn't because they had more control over their dialysis, and could dialyze more often than patients who go to a clinic.

Once in our bedroom, the tech guys turned to Daniel to begin the conversation about the electrical and plumbing requirements. I waited for them to talk to me. They yammered on about outlets. After that, it was the plumbing discussion. The RO machine, intake and output pipes, blah, blah, blah. Then the conversation shifted, and they were discussing the benefits of setting up downstairs on the main floor. Daniel turned to me, "There isn't going to be an end to this, Sam. As you get weaker the stairs are going to be harder."

And there it was. This wasn't just dialysis; this was an exit strategy. We weren't planning for my return to health, we were planning for the best way for me to die. At least Daniel was. He put his arm around my shoulder. "We'll put in a fireplace and some beautiful furniture and it will be a really cozy room. What do you think?" I gritted my teeth and nodded. If that made the most sense then I guessed that was what I would do.

The three men headed down to the basement and I didn't bother joining them. I turned on the computer and paged through my emails, banging my keyboard with force. I was furious and distressed. All three of them had turned this into a simple technical matter, and nobody had thought that I had some feelings involved in where and how I dialyzed. Or even acknowledged how big this was. Daniel came back into the room with some chatter on his lips until he saw my face. He rushed over to hug me.

"It's hard," I whispered as he held me.

"I know," he whispered back.

"It's different if we have it downstairs. It just feels different." I didn't know how to describe the distaste I had for creating a main-floor "sick room." I had visions of a succession of nurses coming to our home, of visitors arriving at the house that would now look like a hospital. I looked at Daniel. "I'm not ready to set up downstairs." And then, with some fierceness, "Don't rush my dying."

"Would you like me to make it work upstairs?" Daniel asked.

"Yes."

And Daniel was off immediately to speak to our team about putting it upstairs. He would support me in whatever I needed. Half an hour later they were gone, and I was still shaking.

37

I DID NOT HAVE an easy start. I had let my body get toxic enough that at first, it didn't know what to do when toxicity was removed. I struggled with blood pressure drops and allergic reactions and felt flattened by each treatment. Shelley had said I would feel better. Where was the better?

"It'll come," Shelley assured me when I lamented to her. "Give it time."

It didn't help that Daniel and I were exhausted just from making the hour drive each way to London three to five times a week. I had to be trained to do the home dialysis. Normally the training was about eight weeks. I took twelve because we lost the first month managing my physical reactions and clearing my mind from the blotto caused by regular bouts of low blood pressure. This wasn't the experience of every dialysis patient; the underlying amyloidosis complicated everything.

—

THESE TWELVE WEEKS were challenging and depressing, but there was a parallel universe where they were wonderful. The previous summer Daniel had closed his business after years of consideration. This was the first summer in almost twenty years that he wasn't stressed and distracted by his work. He was poised to start his master of social work degree that fall, but for the summer he was free to take me to London as often as needed. Zev, seventeen that summer, was busy with his summer job and his friends, so we didn't need to rush back home after dialysis.

We spent hours and hours of time together—driving, dialyzing, getting lunch or dinner after dialysis, going for walks. Similar to when I had my stem-cell transplant, we had a protected space to be together in a quiet way; different this time because we had age on our side. We had been through hard times and come out the other side. Zev was growing up. Daniel had released the stress of running a business and I had years of tai chi that had made me stronger and calmer. All of this time together allowed us to fold around each other again, find a rhythm together, be present together.

Daniel was fully with me, doing the training with me side by side, so that we could do dialysis together. And I needed help. I could not take this on alone. Up until now, I had seen the struggle with this illness as mine. I was the one on the table, I was the one taking the strong medication, I was the one flattened on the couch. I would go to appointments alone; I would go for treatments alone. Daniel sometimes came for important meetings, but I saw it as something he needed to do, not something I needed. Daniel could support me from the outside by cooking for Zev and me, looking after Zev when I couldn't and managing the household. He had deep reservoirs of love that he directed toward me, wanting so badly to make it all better. These were no small feats, but he wasn't in the trenches and I had kept him out, so I could build a safe bubble around me that kept me focused and calm.

But now, I had no choice but to let him in to the intimate process of dialysis. We collaborated to make it work and slowly I let my bubble dissolve. And it was good. It was really good. Our relationship deepened into an entirely new dimension. Throughout all of those years of trying to be strong on my own I had believed that I could do better alone when I could keep my head down and focus. And I had believed that I was relieving Daniel of yet one more burden.

The fundamental principle that I had not understood was that Daniel had *wanted* to help me. In fact, he had been waiting sixteen years to be allowed to look after me in a more significant manner. What I had considered an unwanted burden, he had considered a way to connect and express his love .

I thought back to my father's last words to Daniel: *Take care of Sammy*. Daniel didn't need those words, taking care of people came as naturally to him as breathing. I had seen it in the way he cared for my grandma and the way he attended to my father when he was ill. Daniel would take care of me, wanted to take care of me.

Better if my father had said to *me*, "Let Daniel take care of you." Maybe then it might not have taken me all those years to figure out that by allowing Daniel to help, by giving up some rigid ideas of strength and independence, I would be helping to create something stronger between us.

38

WHEN WE MADE the decision to do home dialysis, we had no idea how much work it would be. There was set-up and take-down, cleaning and maintenance of the machine, managing a number of important decisions each treatment, ordering supplies, ordering medication and, hardest and scariest, inserting the needles into my arm.

The process of needling is called *cannulation*. When I had first heard about it, I doubted I would ever be able to do it. They wanted me to stick needles in myself. I knew it would be part of the whole dialysis thing, but I was in denial until we actually started the training. Early on, before I had to start needling, we met a woman on the elevator who told me that the first few times she needed the nurses to "give her a little something" to relax her enough to actually do it. I was ready to sign up for that. The intrepid nurses, however, were very clever in their methods to train me on the needles.

The first few times, the nurse placed my hand on her hand, so I could feel the movement. She had smooth, cool hands and we coasted into my arm with ease. Then, for a time she placed her hand on my hand. I gave up control and she directed my hand to insert the needle. I watched my hand doing what my brain was resisting. With her sure guidance the needle found its mark. As time passed, she would use a lighter and lighter touch, slowly pulling away until the time when she backed away completely and I almost didn't know it and put the needle in all by myself. In my excitement over my accomplishment, I accidentally pulled the needle back out. Blood spurted everywhere from my forceful fistula. While Daniel and my nurse were hurriedly trying to stop the draining of my life force, I sat there with an idiot grin, so proud of myself.

It took a year before I could relax into the process and two years before I really felt like I had it down. We still made mistakes, but I felt like I was in command of the procedure. I felt better when I dialyzed but was finding dialyzing four or five times a week demanding. It took me almost an hour to get ready and another hour to clean up and disinfect the machine. I would usually dialyze three or four hours. Almost my whole schedule was filled with this six-hour event, which often stretched out because I was fatigued or moving slowly. On top of that I still had other medical tasks and appointments.

Because I was dialyzing at home, I had to manage a small truckload of decisions every day, decisions that became more complex over time. I was, of course, guided in the big picture by my doctor and nurses, who were available any time for consultation. But they weren't on the ground with me and the whole thing was complicated by the underlying amyloidosis. How did I feel on a given day? Was I on my steroid high or low? What was my blood pressure doing? Were my heart irregularities showing up? What should my ideal weight be? And on and on. It's a good thing that I could handle all that complexity, but some days I wished I didn't have to.

—

ANOTHER ISSUE AROSE when I started dialysis: I started accumulating fluid in my belly. When this first started happening, we tried to take the extra fluid out in dialysis. But if we took out too much fluid, my blood pressure would drop to a dangerous level and I would be sent off into a zombie-like state. Thus, dialysis wasn't going to be the hero here.

Nor could I pee out the extra fluid. I was quickly losing kidney function; those wonderful kidneys were forgetting how to make urine.

The solution for the first eighteen months was to have belly taps (known as *paracenteses*). My internist would meet me once a week at the hospital and insert a syringe to draw out the excess fluid. He was very skilled, so it was not as scary as it sounds. Rather it was a relief. We would sometimes take out five or six litres—that's twelve to fifteen pounds of liquid. The hospital was a five-minute, uphill walk from our house. I would drag myself up there in my waddling state and trip home lightly, a changed woman. The paracenteses meant that I could be more cavalier about my fluid intake and could cut down the number of times a week I needed to dialyze. It made the whole thing a little more manageable.

And I needed manageable. I hadn't adapted to dialysis as quickly as I had adapted to the other changes I'd faced throughout my illness. I'm not sure I really adapted at all. Grieving is normal, but I was tired of grieving; tired of going in circles of unhappiness, pining for a life without dialysis. I still needed to figure out how I could claim this life as mine, not just a life that was imposed upon me.

39

I WAS MUMMIFIED IN the sheets, wrapped from head to toe with only my face peeping out. It was more like a straitjacket to contain the convulsing shivers and chattering teeth that had descended upon me when I spiked a fever for no apparent reason. My friend Alison, who had accompanied me to what was supposed to be a simple procedure, kept her hand calmly on my shoulder as she asked the nurse to keep bringing more of the wondrously heated flannel sheets. All I could do was focus on riding the waves of this fever and try desperately to stay afloat as I rose and fell, with Alison's hand as an anchor.

The doctor who had performed the procedure came in, looking at his clipboard. "So, Samantha, I've looked at your ultrasound report and it looks like there are no blood clots. So that means you are safe to go home."

I took a deep breath and waited for him to look at me. Did he not notice that there was something unusual about an outpatient in the fetal position, shrink-wrapped in flannel and sounding like an out-of-control typewriter? There were no comments forthcoming, so I finally said, in the calmest voice I could muster, punctuated with chattering teeth, "I'm concerned about this fever. Frankly I don't think I could move right now the way things are going." I managed not to make a caustic remark about his observation skills. I was good at doctor diplomacy.

He did some mumbling and throat clearing and disappeared, coming back to tell me that yes, this fever was a concern and I would be transferred to the emergency department.

It made sense to go to emergency, but I couldn't help noticing his relief as I was removed from his area of responsibility. What would have happened if I hadn't spoken up?

—

I HAD ALWAYS strived to be a model patient. I wanted to be the friendliest, most engaged, most appreciative patient, as if there were some sort of grade or award. It was built into me. I was raised to be one of the good little Albert girls. During procedures, I would breathe when I was told to, drink whatever awful stuff was put in front of me and not complain when yet another medical student wanted to examine me. I made jokes and engaged the technicians in conversation. In the medical world, being pleasant and co-operative makes life easier. Nurses will often go the extra mile for you if you are agreeable and respectful, which isn't that hard. But perhaps it is, since nurses often remarked to me that my pleasantness was rare. I was not afraid to be a nurse's pet.

I never tried to be a doctor's pet, however. Working with doctors demanded less pleasing and more rigour. It was my life in their hands.

—

UNTIL I BECAME ill, the only doctor I had worked with was my family doctor. When I was first diagnosed with amyloidosis, I needed a hematologist, thus doubling my doctor load to two.

A liver doctor, a heart doctor and a kidney doctor were added over the first few years of my illness. Eventually, because my bone density had been compromised by my long sojourn on the high-dose prednisone, a bone-density doctor was added as well. Then I saw an ophthalmologist because of developing cataracts, also a result of the prednisone. And I continued to see my family doctor for a yearly checkup. That brought me up to seven doctors. My dance card was beginning to fill up:

Later I would add an internist, a respirologist and an infectious disease specialist.

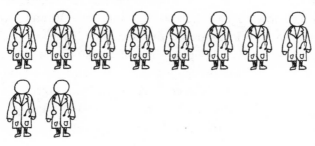

I saw each specialist once or twice a year, except for my hematologist, who I saw every four to six weeks. A visit to a specialist usually was accompanied by blood work or some sort of diagnostic test. Over time, my medical life was becoming increasingly complex and time-consuming.

I had wonderful doctors. They were intelligent, knowledgeable, skilled in their respective fields and kind, and they generally listened to my questions and concerns with respect. But with so many doctors looking after me, I had to navigate the waters between them with tact. Who was in charge on a particular issue? Who should I call when I was in trouble? Who would write the prescription? What if there was a dissenting opinion? What if one of them were to retire? Sometimes I would go to the doctor who I knew would do what I asked or give me the answer I wanted, much like going to the parent you know will say yes to that raise in your allowance.

My sisters should really have been added to this list as they, too, were intimately involved in decision-making. But I had to be careful how I used their opinions: "Well you see, Dr. X, my sister, the rheumatologist, recommended that blah blah blah, and I would really like to go in that direction." I could tell a great deal about doctors by how they reacted to that statement. My sisters are well known and respected in their fields, not sisterly hacks who googled an answer on Web MD. Their opinions were based on medical expertise and a long knowledge of me and my condition. When they have an opinion, it is important that someone listen.

Thus, I was a medical diplomat, of sorts. Negotiating, carrying messages, choosing my words with care. And what country did I represent? The country of me. I was both president and diplomat, the most knowledgeable about me, yet dependent on foreign relations to keep me going.

—

THE REAL FUN would begin when I was admitted to a teaching hospital. There the doctors multiplied like rabbits.

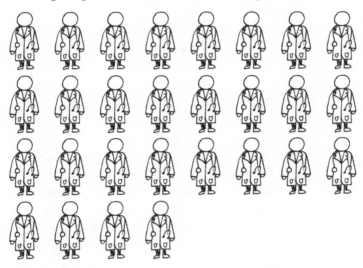

Among the crowds that would come to see me, there were: attending doctors (the one in charge of the team at a given moment), interns, residents, fellows (a doctor in advanced training in a specialty) and, sometimes, medical students. They would come through in herds, one or more herd for each specialty, and my disease branched out into many specialties. A team would walk into my room and I would gird myself for what was to come next. Many were respectful, but sometimes they would talk over me as if I were deaf. "I can hear you," I said to two young residents who were whispering about me at my bedside. And then, "You don't need to yell, I'm not deaf," as they spoke to me like I was the elderly auntie. I felt as cantankerous as a Maggie Smith character.

And while I was a model of co-operation when it came to procedures, I was also a dogged, sometimes annoying, advocate for myself when it came to making decisions about my care. After eighteen years of illness, with the attentiveness I brought to my work as a patient, I knew that mistakes could be made. My best doctors understood and nurtured my active participation and the participation of my other doctors and didn't let ego get in their way. But sometimes new doctors I would meet in the hospital approached me with a "Don't you worry little lady, I've got a handle on it" attitude and I wanted to commit hari-kari.

There are many things new doctors needed to know about my very rare disease both from my hematologist and from me. Most of them had no experience with amyloidosis and didn't know what they didn't know. These doctors were new to me and had no idea how this illness experience was deeply ingrained into my brain and my soul. I was intimately involved in my own care. I had to be because too much happened away from the doctor's office that I had to monitor and manage. I'd had many years to dig deep into the intricacies of the disease both intellectually and physically.

Even my hematologist, a respected doctor who is an international leader in her field, often saw me as a mystery. Amyloid patients used to die faster. Now that patients were living longer, we each experienced unique symptoms and faced specific challenges. There was little that was predictable and much trial and error.

Thus, my hematologist approached my care with openness, careful observation and a system of feedback and monitoring that could tell us if we were making helpful choices. Her decisions and recommendations were based on her extensive knowledge of the illness combined with a long-term relationship with me. This relationship was a critical piece of my care. She understood who I was and carefully selected a course of action based on that information.

When I was in hospital, communication between specialties and even between doctors on the same specialty was problematic, especially at larger hospitals. There were times where there was no coordinated effort of my care. Instead there were piles of specialists wandering through and acting like cowboys. I sent the following email to my family once when I was in hospital and frustrated with the way my care was progressing:

> Here's how the game works. Each doctor is on a team (specialty) with its own secret codes and handshakes. If one sees a member from an opposing team, he or she whistles and looks elsewhere, avoiding interaction at all costs.
>
> The team that orders the most procedures wins. Extra points for creativity. Plus, an extra 100 points if you can split off into a sub-team within your team and run a parallel game. Go team go!

After that particular experience, I developed charts and diagrams to illustrate the pieces of my illness puzzle. I wanted something that could quickly convey the complexity of my life and the sophistication of my understanding. For example, here were some of the things I had to manage at a given moment:

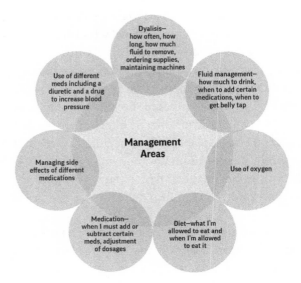

But after developing some of these charts, I wasn't satisfied. They looked dead to me. They were inadequate to truly convey my experience. My medical life was not about creating to-do lists. It didn't fit neatly into an organizational chart. It was an immersion into a relentless whirlwind with profound physical, mental and emotional demands. I could not take any action or make any decision that would not tug on some aspect of my illness. I couldn't ever pretend it wasn't there.

40

I SAT IN MY hospital room trying to get comfortable on the slippery bed. I had been admitted once again—always a depressing course of events. This time, I had developed atrial fibrillation (afib), a heart irregularity that could cause serious complications if not treated. My cardiologist later said that it was likely a result of the amyloid. For now, I was in a different city than my cardiologist and the doctors here were trying to figure out what to do with me.

My nurse came in and handed me one of the little plastic cups used to deliver medication to patients. I looked in to see two little pills that I did not recognize. I looked at the nurse, my favourite one to date. She was a middle-aged woman from Ghana with a gorgeous accent, a common-sense attitude and a huge well of compassion.

"What's this?" I asked.

"You attending doctor has prescribed aspirin." Her lips were tight.

I stared at her. I stared at the pills. I thought about what had led to this decision. The attending probably saw somewhere that the pomalidomide could cause blood clots. She must have thought, "Blood clots? I know what to do, I'll put her on aspirin. That thins the blood!"

But the story didn't end there. My platelets ran low as a side effect of the pomalidomide. Platelets were what helped to stop the bleeding in a person, internally or externally. My hematologist had never put me on any kind of blood thinner because I had my own internal blood thinner, a dearth of platelets. There was no evidence of aspirin in my list of medications. Did the attending think to talk to my hematologist? Did she think to review my blood work?

I looked at my nurse, "I don't think I should take this."

She wasn't allowed to make a recommendation like that, but she ever-so-slightly nodded her head in agreement, took the cup and left the room.

What if I hadn't understood the ins and outs of my care? My nephrologist came to see me later that day and agreed that I had made a wise decision. Later, when I went back to see my regular cardiologist, he was shocked that the attending doctor had prescribed aspirin and said that the results could have been catastrophic. Bleeding from a cut is one thing, but bleeding internally with low platelets and a blood thinner could have easily led to my demise.

That was one decision at one moment. I made decisions all day every day that required my attention. Decisions about dialysis, about medications, about diet.

If new doctors were involved in my care in the hospital, I had to ensure that they were making good decisions. Once I literally put the brakes on the stretcher that was to take me for what I thought was an unnecessary MRI. "Wait a minute, *why* does the neurology attending want me to have another MRI?" While I seemed like a troublemaker in the moment, my choice was later vindicated by several doctors who agreed the test was, indeed, unnecessary. I questioned every new medication and consulted with my regular doctors when necessary. I didn't like being the troublemaker. And I wasn't trying to get out of taking these medications. But after the aspirin episode I knew I had to double-check every prescription and make sure that somebody hadn't made a dangerous decision without knowing all of the information.

The sheer magnitude of my medical life was daunting, fatiguing, relentless and always in danger of being challenged. I had to be hyper-aware every minute, the way an air traffic controller can never let their attention drift. And, like an air traffic controller, my inattention could, in some cases, lead to death. My death. Never, ever could I look away.

Amyloidosis had been all-pervasive before, but there had still been spaces in which I could fit a life. Dialysis oozed in and filled most of those spaces, leaving no cracks. I could never let my attention wander. To make matters worse, new health issues kept springing up like moles in the whack-a-mole, each one bringing new doctors, new medications and new routines. Cataracts, atrial fibrillation, hernia, infections, cryptococcal meningitis.

I had to be cautious with how much fluid I took in every day because everything that went in had to come out through dialysis, which had its limits. I couldn't indulge in a big glass of lemonade on a hot and sweaty day. I drank sparingly, spreading out my allocated amount throughout the day.

Sometimes I would watch Daniel guzzling glass after glass of water and would be sick with jealousy. I thought about the feeling of a cool flow of water drizzling down my throat. I wanted to feel that sweet moment of letting go of my worry, of the need to control every action; I imagined it would feel like letting oneself float in a lake with closed eyes, face to the sun.

41

TURNING FIFTY, for me, was dope. No other way to say it. I loved turning fifty and being fifty. My first thought on my birthday was, "Yes, I made it! High five!" There was more to my enjoyment of fifty than merely surviving, however. At fifty, I was old enough to have relationships that were, themselves, twenty and thirty years old. That length of time provided depth and richness that I never would have imagined. And somehow turning fifty gave me certain superpowers of perception. And not only in my relationships; I felt like everything and everyone I paid attention to revealed something deeper and richer. It was as if I was seeing things in their entirety and not just in pieces. And it wasn't the drugs.

—

DANIEL AND I decided to have a party. It was a milestone year. Daniel also was turning fifty and Zev had turned eighteen. Zev had graduated from high school and Daniel had graduated with a masters of social work. My first hematologist had suggested that seven years was the average time people survived with amyloidosis. At seven years we'd had a giant bonfire party. Now it was seventeen years. Another good reason to celebrate. On top of all of that, 2017 marked the twenty-fifth anniversary of that fateful day I had met Daniel and thought, "Here's someone I'm not going to like."

We decided it was cause for a party. Friends and relatives came from near and far. This was a full family celebration; at least I thought it was.

—

I LEANED MY forehead in towards Daniel's and gave him a kiss. "Daniel, I feel bad. I hardly said anything in my speech about you, but your speech was almost entirely about me!" We had found a quiet corner to talk among the crowds of people dancing to the tropical sounds of the marimba band and eating tiny empanadas and other quick grab foods. The colourful lanterns dotting the air above the dance floor cast a romantic edge on the exposed brick and original wood of the factory that had once been there. It was exactly the kind of party I had wanted.

In my speech I had hoped to honour those who were there and those who were not. I had wanted to express how much it meant to us to have all of them in our lives. Daniel had talked about me and my character (stubborn) that had helped me to live this long. It was a beautiful speech and I was embarrassed that I hadn't talked more about him.

"Well, it's really your party," Daniel said.

"Whoa. My party?!!" I snapped. "Look at all of the things we're celebrating. I thought we had decided this together and you were into it."

"Well, you wanted a party, so I said I wanted one too, so you would be happy." He shrugged his shoulders and offered me the sweet look of a child discovered with his hand in the candy dish.

Zev was standing nearby, so I dragged him in.

"Zev, did you want to have this party? It's your celebration too."

Zev looked at the floor. "Well, not really. I mean, I'm having a lot of fun. But I didn't want a party that was about me."

"Well, I didn't need to have a party," I snarked to Daniel. I was now feeling guilty about the money we had spent and all the work and stress I had put Daniel and Zev through. I received plenty of attention all the time. It was always about me. This time, I had wanted to celebrate all of us. Zev, hearing the tone in my voice, slid away from us and headed for the food.

"But look how many people came—how many wanted to come. Rena came all the way from Timmins. You haven't seen her in years. You couldn't have kept Aunt Cheryl away. Ian came from Winnipeg—even though you didn't invite him! Ellie and Jerry came all the way from California. Aunt Susie wanted to come and be here. I could go on and on. They all wanted a reason to come to see you."

"I don't know..." I muttered.

"Sam, remember all the times we thought you were going to die? And then you were so sick when you started dialysis. You can't travel to see them anymore. You haven't been to the Thanksgiving gathering in years. You haven't been able to go on family vacations. Everyone is thrilled to come to this party. Really, you're the only person in the room that doesn't understand that the party is about *you*." He put his arm around me and kissed me and then rubbed my back, as if he was taming a wild animal. He leaned in and whispered, "This is what I wanted. Don't worry about me."

There was a release and I felt as if I was melting inside. I turned away to wipe my eyes and blow my nose. I allowed my guilt and anxiety to dissipate into the warm, loving air of the party. Okay, it was about me. But it was also about everyone that had come. That's what I had been trying to convey in my speech.

Daniel had found a bowl of warm olives and we munched on these as we turned to take in the room. It was a potluck mix of friends and family from different parts of our lives. There were relatives galore: our immediate families; nearby relatives that we saw with some regularity; and the far-away relatives that we only saw for the big events.

I saw my mother in conversation with a relative from Winnipeg. I could hear her laughter from across the room. Like my dad and me, she laughed full on with her head thrown back. I loved seeing that act of release and enjoyment so much more than the expression of tight worry she wore in hospital waiting rooms.

Barbara and Leon, Daniel's parents, were there working the room, getting to know our friends and my family. Their infinite curiosity pushed them on to meet new people and learn about their lives. And they remembered what they learned and told us more about our friends than we had ever known.

There were friends from my undergraduate years and from both of my graduate programs. Friends from my tai chi community, the local Jewish community and our synagogue. Friends we'd grown with from youth to middle age and friends with whom we'd only connected recently. There were old neighbours and previous clients of Daniel's.

These important people from different parts of our lives were mingling and spinning their own independent webs of connection with each other. Daniel was right. I could let the party be about me. But even though I had called the gathering, I wasn't at the centre. There was no centre, just a continually growing set of connections. Watching the activity in the room was like being able to see love manifest and it was good.

PART EIGHT

16.   17.

42

SIX MONTHS AFTER our party, everything changed.
I was in hospital. Again. This time with a serious
infection. Again. The drugs I had been given for my
infection had caused my blood pressure to drop, so I was
given extra saline. Then I had to drink the fluid to prepare for
two CT scans. I was supersaturated and impossibly swollen.
My legs were like tree trunks that wouldn't bend, my belly
was massive, nine months pregnant with triplets, my hands
were swollen like sausages. One day, I was trapped on the
toilet, unable to lift my mammoth body up without the help
of a strong nurse.

This time there were no distractions, no sequestering
myself away. I was in hospital, deteriorated, trying to imagine how this would end.

The doctors tried to do a paracentesis, a belly tap, but
this was no longer an option. The pockets in my abdomen
were too small, the result of adhesions from abdominal surgery that had been performed the previous fall. The fluid
had moved into the tissue, making it almost impossible to
extract. Without a way to remove fluid, I imagined I would
keep expanding, the way Violet Beauregarde expanded into
a giant blueberry in *Charlie and the Chocolate Factory*.

I had never been so miserable. If I lay down, a boulder would set itself on my chest and I felt the terror of not being able to breathe. If I slept sitting up, my head would hang over my chest, stressing my neck and back, despite all my attempts to prop it up. The hospital bed was impossible, so they brought me one of their special blow-up beds, which was slippery. I would find myself pooled at the centre of the mattress, unable to get enough purchase to uncurl myself into a more comfortable position. There was some relief in sitting in my dialysis chair that Daniel had brought from home, but I still could not recline very far before the weight in my chest caused a halt.

I needed oxygen to help me breathe with some ease. My appetite disappeared. The pressure on my stomach meant that even if I was hungry, I could only take in a bit of food before the additional pressure made me feel nauseated. My stretched skin was itchy and raw. Getting my lumbering body in and out of the chair or bed was a major event.

Sleep was impossible; my discomfort never took a break. When it was three in the morning and I had all the hours behind me and all the hours ahead and no way to find relief, I felt like a bird in cupped hands—fluttering my wings, helpless to do anything, frantic. For so many years I had fought to stay alive and fought to be healthy. I might have responded to changes with initial reluctance, but with time, I was able to adapt. There had been extremely hard times, but this was something different. I had never been in such physical distress, with no hope of improvement. When I thought of continuing to live like this my heart rate would rise and I would begin to sweat with panic. In the hospital, during those restless and hopeless nights, I would whisper to myself, "I can't do this anymore. I just can't do this anymore."

—

"IF THERE'S ANYTHING you want to say to anybody, I would suggest doing it sooner rather than later." The palliative doctor was a soft-spoken woman whose kind eyes were framed by long curly hair that was pleasantly out of control. She walked us through our situation with both discretion and directness. She had been briefed on my case and agreed that I might return to relative health or my health could deteriorate very quickly. I had been plagued with infection after infection and one more might do me in. In addition, there was no resolution yet to the accumulation of fluid in my enormous body.

Daniel and I sat clutching each other's hands, sniffling, the tears streaming at different moments. The doctor laid out our options and walked us through a number of decisions that we had to make. She apprised us of the support services we could ask for once I was home. She told us what we might expect as the end came closer. We told the doctor about Zev and cried some more. We had a few questions for her and then there was no more to say.

For me, there was catharsis in hearing the doctor confirm my sense that I was approaching the end. That was my reality in that moment, but those around me were still talking about survival. I needed Daniel to hear from a professional that things were grave.

The intensity of the situation took my breath away. We were talking about dying, really dying. Really being in this world no more. And for the first time I welcomed this possibility. For the first time I was in such bad shape that the idea of not existing outweighed the pain of leaving all the people I loved so much, of leaving the beautiful parts of this world and leaving unfinished business.

I asked Daniel if I could speak to the doctor alone. He looked a question but left us.

"I'm struggling..." I couldn't talk without weeping. The doctor pushed more tissues my way.

"Take your time."

"I'm struggling because I know that for Daniel, all that matters is to keep me alive. Of course it does. We want to be together in this world for as long as possible. It's always been that way. But whether it's on purpose or because his vision is limited, he can't see that being alive is not all that matters. If this is what I can expect from the future," I opened my arms to display my weighted body, "I can't do it. I just can't do it. It terrifies me to think about surviving in this state." I put my head down on the table. Maybe I could eliminate fluid through the waterfall of tears. The doctor rubbed my back. What was there for her to say?

—

I FELT CLEAR and calm after meeting with the palliative doctor. I was ready. I felt no need to hide away. I wanted to speak to the people I loved. I wanted to say goodbye. Shortly after that meeting, the doctors sent me home.

I sent communiqués to my nearest and dearest. I hosted small groups of friends on my better days to say goodbye. I would sit in the centre of the group with my great lumbering form and make bad jokes about dying, causing those there to squirm and study the art on the wall. I started giving away some of my things and labelling other things that were to be wrapped up and given later.

Zev came home, having finished exams. I sat him down to tell him everything. But this time was very different from the time I spoke to him over milkshakes by the river. Getting the words out was not the hard part, it was watching the pain. I wondered now about what it was like for my father to tell me he was dying. I was not much older than Zev when my father and I had had our conversation.

I spent time talking with my mother. I knew that my death must have been unbearable for her to contemplate. I couldn't know what the years of worrying about me had done to her. But I did know that if it had been Zev that was ill with an incurable, life-threatening disease, the stress would have emptied me until I was hollow and ready to crack. I told my mother that I was not afraid and that I was ready. It was a privileged time to speak so openly with her.

I spent time connecting with my sisters and their spouses, with Barbara and Leon, with Sandra.

I reflected on the timing of my dying. I had survived far longer than anyone expected. I was grateful for the extra years that had allowed me to watch Zev grow up and had given Daniel and me the space to deepen our relationship. But the timing of our deaths is arbitrary. And there is never enough time. There's always that one more thing you don't want to miss. I was curious and eager to see how Zev would grow his life and navigate the world. I wanted to watch the crinkles deepen around Daniel's eyes, those eyes that had captured my heart so many years earlier, those eyes that still were so dear to me. I didn't want to miss a thing. And yet, here I was, trapped in this impossible body approaching a life I couldn't live with. How much more could I tolerate?

Opening night of the Stratford Festival, June 2019. Zev is twenty years old and I am on a steroid high and in fine form.

—

IN THE VELVET hours of one long night, wakefulness interspersed with moments of sleep; thoughts interspersed with dreams. My wobbly mind floated through my life, trying to grasp at my accomplishments. What had I actually done? What was I leaving behind? My dad's voice repeated in my head, "I have no regrets... no regrets... no regrets." His had been a life of love, although he wouldn't have expressed it that way.

I thought back to our party from the previous summer. I remembered all the love that had been represented there that night; the web of interconnections that was almost visible with firing synapses. People laughing, connecting, creating.

I had been lucky enough to participate in many loving relationships and each one generated an independent exhalation of love into the atmosphere that joined up with the rest of the love in the world, as if there was a giant, global soup pot of love. And the soup pot was always there and would carry on after we were gone. And all I needed to know, to feel like my life had value, was that I had somehow contributed a little bit of love to the soup.

The next day I tried to explain my soup pot to Daniel and my mother and my friends. It reminded me of the time I had been sure that our neighbour's house had a secret tunnel leading away from her basement—an image I was sure was real, but which had come to me in a dream.

"It's okay," I kept saying to my bewildered loved ones. "I'm part of the soup and you are too and one day you'll also be gone, but the love we created will still carry on." It had sounded sane and clear in the middle of the night. In the daylight it sounded whacky. I agreed that it sounded whacky, but in my mind, I knew it was real in its own way.

I truly didn't know if my death was imminent. I had always come back from the edge just in time. I could not see how we would get out of this one, but the possibility was there. Whether I survived or not, the momentum of all that love would carry on with or without me. That would be my legacy. That would make it all worth it. No regrets.

AFTERWORD

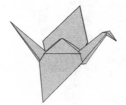

The Girl With the Backpack

I T'S HARD TO remember there was a time when I was sturdy and strong, with the capacity to garden all day and party all night. Energy was not something that had to be meted out with miserly caution. I was an image of fine, youthful health.

I gaze at the picture that captures this golden time, the time before everything changed. It was taken the summer before Zev was born; the summer Daniel and I both turned thirty-one. We had embarked on a canoe trip deep into the wilderness away from the comforts of beds, running water and flush toilets.

"Is that really you?" Zev, now a teenager, asks, looking over my shoulder at the snapshot. The girl in the picture sports an immense backpack, cinched tight around her narrow waist. She squints out from under her hat with a resigned smile.

"Yup."

"But I thought you always had a big belly."

Even I'm skeptical. It does, indeed, feel like I've always been ill. Zev has only ever known the mama with the big belly and awkward lap, who was too tired to play. It reassures me to reach further back in time and know that I was once this girl who had the energy and sense of adventure to march off to seek the peace of the deep wilderness, accompanied only by her young husband and a heavy backpack.

I look hopelessly young in the picture, still girlish. At the time, I didn't really believe in my own beauty. I felt too skinny, too flat-chested, too weak. I used to tell Daniel, sometimes joking, sometimes in tears, that he should have married a big, blonde, athletic Scandinavian girl who could keep up with him.

Now I want to shake that girl in the picture and tell her to appreciate her skinny body that was, in reality, lithe and animated. I want to tell her not to be afraid when the illness comes; she will grow the strength she needs.

—

"DO WE HAVE to take the picture right now?" I whine to Daniel.

I'm grubby and tired and the three-kilometre portage looms over me. My pack is loaded and I'm ready to go.

A portage is both the bane and the brilliance of a canoe trip. To reach remote lakes in the interior, it's necessary to navigate the land that joins lake to lake. To cross a portage, all is lifted out of the water—packs, paddles and canoes— and borne aloft to the next lake.

The packs are inevitably heavy, really heavy, meant to be hauled by canoe, not by people. The paths can seem endless and the heat more cloying in the still woods than on the water. While crossing the portages, I long to be free of my burden and out again on the water where I can close my eyes, feel the wind caress my face and sniff the crisp lake air like a dog hanging out of a car window.

The hard work of the portage is the offering that allows us, in exchange, to immerse ourselves in a landscape empty of the whine of engines, the blare of music and the ringing of phones. So, portages it is. But this is the longest one I've ever tackled.

"C'mon Daniel. Let's get going. This is heavy."

"This will only take a minute."

"But I'm sure I look terrible."

Daniel smiles at me, "You look beautiful. C'mon, how often have you done a three-kilometre portage? Look at that huge pack you're wearing. Don't you want to remember this moment?"

I set a tolerant smile on my face to please Daniel and he captures his picture. I set the lifejackets and water bottles over my pack and pick up the paddles. Daniel kisses me and ensures my pack is adjusted before he gathers up the other pack and the canoe. He smiles at me and sets off down the trail. I follow, but I can't keep up to his fast march, so he's out of sight within the first five minutes. I let myself slow down and settle in for the long hike.

I try to be in the present and enjoy the tapestry of a million shades of green and the penetrating coniferous scent of the pines. I'm not indifferent to the beauty of my surroundings, but it's hard for me to look past my sore back, tired feet and itchy bites. I'm easily distracted from wonder by my discomforts. By the time I approach the end of the trail I'm down to a trudge. I see the lake slip through the trees until an expanse of welcoming cool water and big sky opens its arms to me. Reenergized, I quicken my step.

Arriving at the edge of the lake, I unbuckle the tight straps and drop the pack. Daniel naps under a nearby tree, and I let him sleep. I'm exhausted, sweaty, itchy and hungry, but now none of that matters. I've conquered the three-kilometre portage, my biggest physical challenge to date.

Off come my shoes and damp socks. My feet emerge, hot and sweaty, to dip in and claim the waters of Great Mountain Lake. The sounds are sharper here, the pictures crisper, the smells deeper.

A light breeze wisps through the hair on my arms and raises ripples on the deep green lake, causing the loons to gently bob up and down and the water grasses to sway as if an invisible conductor keeps them in time. Coniferous trees stand guard around the edge of the lake, their prickly green–blackness contrasting with the soft fresh green of the deciduous trees. Magnificent outcroppings of Canadian Shield jut out pink, white and golden.

I close my eyes and inhale, filling my lungs and letting my body circulate this precious air out to the far reaches of my body.

Once we've canoed to our campsite and set up for the night, I take off for the water. I slide into the sweet, silky, cold lake water, all clothing abandoned. I want the blessing of this water. I immerse myself, once, twice, three times. And then I fly, free, feeling the water cleanse me of the last vestiges of city life. Then I float, face up to the sun, with my eyes closed, sculling enough to keep from sinking. I am where I most want to be. The sound of the lake fills my ears. The water enfolds me, rocks me and soothes me.

Daniel joins me in the lake. As he swims, his eyes are steady on me; those hazel eyes that crinkle up with love, enough love to fill a lake. This is what we have come for, this time to twine together in the quiet noise of the forest. Each night of this trip, as we sit in the firelight, snug together on a rock or a log, drinking our tea, we spin out our future.

"...When we have kids, we could do this trip with them ..."

"...Do you think Frank is serious about selling the house to us...?"

"...Maybe in ten years we can take longer summer vacations..."

"... so next summer we might have a baby!!"

Our faces, lit by firelight, float close together in the darkness as we shape a seamless journey on a long, smooth road.

EPILOGUE

BY DANIEL SHOAG

L ET'S GO TURTLE hunting." Getting Sam out of the house
could be hard, but I could usually entice her with
turtles.

Three years had passed since she had been so terribly
ill. Though she was often tired, we had many good times.
When she had the energy, Sam cooked wonderful meals and
chatted with friends. She made pickles. And, at her request,
I painted a downstairs room her favourite sunny yellow and
she filled it with vibrantly coloured works of art. Then we
moved the dialysis machine downstairs so our bedroom
could be a sanctuary again.

Sam needed a lot of rest, but she could usually muster the
strength for turtle hunting. I took her arm and we made our
way slowly to the river across the street.

We began talking about the time when she was in so much
pain and discomfort that she wasn't sure she could go on.

"If you had to come up with a name for that, the feeling
of being so hopeless and in pain, what would it be?" I was
taking a course on narrative therapy and Sam was very kindly
letting me practice my therapy skills on her.

"You know, I have come to think of that as the Grey Zone. I am on a desolate windswept prairie. All I can see, for miles around, is dead grass blowing in a November wind. Steel-coloured clouds in the sky. I'm completely alone. There is no hope of ever finding my way out. I don't ever want to go back there." We walked downhill and left that topic behind.

When we reached the river, Sam smiled with delight and chided me lovingly as she spotted the first turtle. "It's so pretty out!" she said. "Aren't we lucky? We have our beautiful home by the river, Zev, our family and friends, good food. My god, things could be so much worse."

"We are lucky, indeed," I said and watched her smiling, her hair reflecting red in the setting sun. "So, what would you call *this* feeling?"

She hummed as she thought. "It would have to describe the comfortable feeling I have when I walk in the door of our home. We have worked through a lot, you and I, and we have come to this wonderful place in our relationship. You can feel it in our home. People comment on it when they arrive." She smiled. "I think I would call it 'Love House.' I know it sounds kind of cheesy, but it captures that feeling so well. Yes, Love House." She put her arm in mine and we looked out across the water hoping to spot more turtles.

———

"DANIEL, I NEED help." I bolted up the stairs, as I had a thousand times before. "I need to get to the washroom, but I don't have the energy."

"Sure, my love, no problem. Let me help you."

I spent the night tending to her, my body heavy with fatigue by the time the sun rose. I could only imagine how she felt. "There is no way you can dialyze at home today, and I can't get you to the hospital on my own. Sam, I think we need to call an ambulance." Due to Covid-19, the global pandemic that had been isolating us from the world for the past year and a half, I was not allowed in the ambulance or the hospital, so I waved her a quick goodbye and headed back inside for a nap before starting my day at work. I wasn't too worried. We had been here many times before.

A few hours later, I was interrupted by a call from the hospital. "Daniel, your wife is very ill. You need to come now." I dropped what I was doing and ran up the hill to the hospital. I was immediately let into Sam's room. Machines beeped as the nurses tended to her. She did not look well.

The emerge doc entered. "Sam's situation is dire." This sounded familiar, but more worrying this time. "If Sam does not have surgery immediately, she will die. Even if we do surgery, there is a chance she may not survive."

We had a few minutes before they wheeled Sam away. "Daniel, will you call Zev?"

I dialed his number, then listened as she spoke with our son.

"Zev, I am in hospital. I am really sick. I actually might not survive this time." They were both crying. "This is sad, I know, but it is not a tragedy. I've had a good life. It just might be my time to go." They cried for a while longer, then I heard Zev tell her about a meal he had made the other night. Nothing special. Pasta with a simple tomato sauce. He knew food was important to her and that she would appreciate hearing about his cooking. She was a bit loopy on drugs, but the sound of love in her voice as she asked him about the meal stood out. Even in this moment she was caring for others.

"I'm going to miss you, Mama."

"I'm going to miss you too, my love."

Sam spoke to my parents, then asked me to phone her mother. By this time her voice was barely a whisper. They murmured unintelligible words of sorrow and love and comfort to one another and, after they said their last goodbye, Sam asked for the phone back to speak with her mom once more.

"I love you, Mama."

———

SAM DID SURVIVE the surgery, but she was on the edge of death.

With Sam's sisters and mother on the phone, we listened as the surgeon and ICU doctor spoke with us. "Her situation is very complex. She is in septic shock, the surgery was only partially successful, and she will need many more. And she has something I have never seen before, gas in the wall of her heart. We can try to keep her alive, but she will need to be transferred to the ICU in London immediately. We have an ambulance waiting. You need to decide."

Her state was so serious they would need to send three nurses and a doctor in the ambulance to try to keep her alive for the journey. "She could require months in the ICU. Normally, we would allow visitors, but these are not normal times. You would not be allowed in to see her, even if she was dying. With Covid cases rising, there is a chance the ICU could fill up with people who are more likely to survive than she is. I am not sure what would happen in that case..."

I listened as they discussed the intricacies of Sam's condition.

The family and I talked but did not come to a decision. Overwhelmed with grief, I thought of Sam's wishes and the doctor's words: "You need to decide."

"What are the chances Sam will recover?"

The doctor spoke, but what I noticed most was the way he shook his head.

This was not a decision for me to make on my own. Fortunately, our dear friend Liora, a doctor, had arrived. With her comforting presence by my side, I phoned Sam's mom. We went over the details of Sam's condition again and again, and I told her that if she wished for Sam to go to London, that is what we would do. Part of me wanted her to tell me that we needed to keep trying at all costs. But in our hearts, we both knew this wasn't an option. There was a good chance Sam would die in the ambulance, or alone in a hallway in the London hospital. And if she did survive, she would be so compromised there would be no real life for her. That's not what she would have wanted.

We were in tears, but by the time we finished speaking, we knew it was time to let her go.

I would stay with Sam in the hospital in Stratford and be with her to the end.

My chest was so tight I could hardly breathe. My god, what had we done?

I realized I could stay self-absorbed, or I could be there with Sam. I knew I had to let the anxiety go. I willed myself to be fully engaged with her. And, as strange as it sounds, it was also a moment of tremendous beauty. I had one last time to connect with my wife. To tend to her, care for her, hold her, and let her know that she was loved.

I whispered words of love and sang to her the song our friends sang to us as we walked up the hill towards our wedding. I held her hands and kissed her forehead as she slipped away.

—

BECAUSE OF THE pandemic, only ten people were allowed at Sam's funeral. Immediate family, of course, and Sandra. Each of us told a story that reflected how our lives had been enriched by being in Sam's orbit. As the rabbi recited prayers, I glanced up from the simple wooden casket our friend Paul had built. Word had gotten out. There, scattered throughout the cemetery, were our friends, gathered in small groups, grieving with us and supporting us. I could feel Sam's presence there too, smiling her beautiful smile and enveloping us with her love.

SAM'S
FIELD NOTES

FIELD NOTE 1

Denise's Dilled Beans

Ingredients
1 bushel (24 pounds) green beans
whole mustard seed
dill seed
30 cloves garlic, each one cut in two
crushed red pepper (optional)
distilled white vinegar
water
salt
sugar

Method
1. Thoroughly wash beans. Trim to fit, standing, in pint or half-pint jars. Use the youngest, slimmest beans you can find (that are still developed). It's not worth it to put in older beans; they are not as tender or flavourful.

2. To each jar add:
   ½ tsp whole mustard seed
   ½–1½ tsp dill seed
   1 clove garlic
   ¼ tsp crushed red pepper (optional)

3. Combine and boil (this quantity of syrup will fill 7 pint jars):
   5 cups distilled white vinegar
   5 cups water
   ½ cup salt
   ¼ cup sugar

4. Pour hot syrup into jars within half-inch of the lid. Screw lids on lightly.

5. Process 8 minutes in boiling water bath. Make sure each jar seals.

6. Store in cool place and wait at least 8 weeks before eating.

Yield: 6–7 pints

Notes:
Works very nicely with cucumbers to make a flavourful pickle. Cauliflower, hot peppers or carrots can also be pickled this way.

1 bushel of green beans (a generous bushel) will make approximately 27 jars of dilled beans.

FIELD NOTE 2

Roberta's Chicken Soup

Ingredients
Assorted chicken pieces from a pullet or kosher roasting/
frying hen
3 onions
5 carrots, scraped
5 stalks of celery (leaves included)
salt, peppercorns, sugar, dried parsley flakes, garlic powder

Method
1. Cover chicken with water in a large pot and bring to a boil, then reduce to a simmer.

2. Add 1–2 Tbsp salt, 5–6 peppercorns, a pinch of sugar, all of the vegetables

3. Top with dried parsley and let simmer for 6 to 8 hours.

4. Remove chicken and vegetables (reserve a bit of each for table soup if you want).

5. Put soup through sieve, pressing hard on remaining vegetables to get every drop of soup out.

6. Refrigerate until fully cooled.

7. Remove fat from top of cooled soup.

8. Before serving, add some garlic powder and taste for salt.

 Scan the QR code for a more detailed description of how to make this soup and to watch my video on YouTube.

FIELD NOTE 3

The Farmerette

I only recently uncovered a picture of a farmerette. Most of the documents I had been finding used the word to refer to a young female farmer—the equivalent of a Land Girl. I then found some photos of the "farmerettes" in the Broadway musical Guys and Dolls, but was fairly certain this was not what my grandma had in mind.

After great sleuthing I found a catalogue with farmerette knickerbockers for girls, and an article that mentioned farmerette overalls. These must be what the cover star for the 1928 pop song "Farmerette" is wearing.

I'm still trying to locate a definitive picture of what was called a "farmerette" either in Winnipeg between 1904 and 1928 or in Vancouver after 1928.

FIELD NOTE 4

My Bookshelf

I read many books about people living with illness, but only a select few sat on my desk as both reference and inspiration:

Broyard, Anatole. *Intoxicated by my Illness.* Fawcett Columbine, 1992.

Engelberg, Miriam. *Cancer Made Me a Shallower Person: A Memoir in Comics.* Harper Perennial, 2006.

Frank, Arthur W. *At the Will of the Body: Reflections on Illness.* First Mariner Books, 1992.

Harrison, Teva. *In-Between Days.* Anansi Press, 2016.

Kalanithi, Paul. *When Breath Becomes Air.* Corcovado, 2016.

Norton, Meredith. *Lopsided: A Memoir.* Penguin, 2009.

O'Farrell, Maggie. *I Am, I Am, I Am: Seventeen Brushes with Death.* Knopf Canada, 2018.

The following two books provided profound perspectives on meaning-making and finding purpose and helped me through some hard times:

Frankl, Viktor E. *Man's Search for Meaning.* Beacon Press, 1959.

Kinew, Wab. *The Reason You Walk.* Viking Canada, 2015.

My favourite books about craft were:

Fish, Stanley. *How to Write a Sentence: And How to Read One.* Harper, 2012.

Patchett, Ann. *This is the Story of a Happy Marriage.* Harper Collins, 2013.

Pinker, Steven. *The Sense of Style: The Thinking Person's Guide to Writing in the 21ˢᵗ Century.* Viking Penguin, 2014.

Thomas, Abigail. *Thinking About Memoir.* Sterling, 2008.

FIELD NOTE 5

O Canada

While I was preparing for my stem-cell transplant I found a self-help book called *Your Stem-Cell Transplant and You* (or something very like it). It walked through the mechanics of a transplant and laid out some expectations of what I might experience.

One of the last chapters was about negotiating this procedure with your insurance company. At that time (2000), the estimated cost of a transplant in the United States was $200,000. It appeared that there were some scenarios where insurance would not cover this cost.

Here in Canada, I never had to spend a minute thinking about the cost. In fact, I remember being a little indignant that I had to pay for a phone in my room. I didn't have to figure out how to pay for the transplant, I didn't have to worry that one little loophole might bankrupt us. I didn't have to choose between my health and my home.

The transplant was just the beginning. I shudder to think about how twenty years of illness might have played out in a country that didn't commit to looking after all of its sick citizens. I am always grateful for the care that I have received, with excellent doctors, nurses and support staff.

It is an imperfect system, but I'm proud that we, as a country, made the decision and continue to make the decision, to look after each other.

ACKNOWLEDGMENTS

IT TAKES A village to raise a book. My village is wide and deep. Without my medical team I would not be here to write this book. I am grateful to the Canadian medical system that has funded my health care. Thank you to the many doctors, nurses and support workers, so many of you, that have cared for me with respect and grace. A special thank you to Dr. Donna Reece, who leads my medical team. I cannot express enough gratitude for her skill, her fierceness, her kindness and her respect. Also, thank you to her assistant, Lani Endo, who accomplishes the miraculous when the need is great.

The Fung Loy Kok Institute of Taoism was founded in 1970 by a Taoist monk named Master Moy Lin Shin. I would have been truly lost without this volunteer-run, charitable organization and the practice of the Taoist arts. My gratitude to Master Moy for training and inspiring people and for establishing a structure that would live on after his death, carrying forward his mission of compassion. Similarly, my profound thanks to those who have worked so hard to carry on his vision to keep the organization moving forward. I have received generous instruction and support from many people in the organization—all done from the heart.

Without my writing team, there would be no book. A thank you to my instructors, support staff and peers at the UBC Creative Writing Program for helping me grow into the writer that I am now.

Wayne Grady, who told me to write to find the story, Nancy Lee, who did not freak out when I said, "I'm dying, I need to finish my thesis now!" and who taught me a tremendous amount about teaching. I was fortunate enough to be in classes with Charlotte Gill for two consecutive years and those two years were crucial for my writing development under her guidance. She had the patience to tell me the same things over and over again until some of it sank in and she always made me believe I had the capacity to do better. Maureen Medved, my advisor, challenged me to dig deeper and write leaner. She understood my writing and my situation enough to help get me through the final stages of the degree.

There are a few heroic souls who helped during the long process and although it is impossible to list them all here, I would like to mention a few:

- I don't know if there would have been a book without Alison Wearing. Her experience and skill made her a perceptive editor. Her constancy and kindness allowed her to talk me down off the ledge more than once. Her friendship buoyed me up.

- Sandra Dunn listened to the same pieces over hours and hours together, always with an essential piece of feedback. She made me feel as if this book was something that people might want to read. Her friendship, deep and wide, enduring so long, always nourishes me.

- Liora Steele, both a dear friend and a doctor, was always generous about providing a medical opinion or helping out when needed.

- Marsha Eberhardt has been a constant in giving me support and dragging me out to tai chi events, even when I did not think I had the energy to go.

- Jenn Wells has been a beacon for me. Aside from giving me a beautiful friendship, she has given my book far more attention than it deserves, walking into my life at critical moments to listen to a scene or to do a monster proofread and provide generous feedback.

- Many friends have read all or part of the book or provided other kinds of support that helped my writing: Sherri Fraser, Al Voort, Jacob Grodzinski, Cheryl Pinkus, Sara Hershenson, Pat Quigley, Vicki Loss, Elisabet Veenema and Daniel Hershfield. Senya Prescott edited with enthusiasm and encouragement. Julie Sedivy helped me find my way in the forest. I am sure there are many of you that I have missed. Know that I love you.

My family...

- My mother, Roberta—our umbilical connection trumps chicken soup any day. But the chicken soup is pretty exceptional. You are a deep source of everything. As I've said before, I may tug at the connection, but I never stray too far.

- I wish I could tell my father, Henry Albert, how much he taught me about dying and about living. It's been a lifetime since he passed away and I am not that far away from the age that he was when he died, yet the more I write about him, the more present he becomes in my life.

- The A team: Lori and Shelley, my remarkable sisters who chose their partners, Joel and Cindy, with care. I am fortunate in having close and loving relationships with my sisters and their families. Everyone on my team has bent over backwards over the years to help me. I'm sure there were nights of lying awake worrying over me, and I wish I could take those away.

- Hannah, Elan, Seth and Faye for being your own wonderful selves and reminding me of renewal and the future.

- My in-laws, Barbara and Leon Shoag. You have supported us in so many ways, most importantly in your constant love, generosity and encouragement. Right from the beginning, you believed I would write a book.

- Zev, I am so proud of the man you have become. You have only ever been encouraging about my writing. Thank you for letting me write about you.

- Daniel, my love, you got more sickness than health in our deal. You have not wavered once in encouraging my writing. Not only did you look after me in sickness, you listened to my writing over and over again during the ten years that this took to come to fruition.

Samantha Albert, August 11, 2019

MOST BOOKS HAVE one acknowledgement. This book has two. Sam died before this book was published, so it was left up to Sam's mom, Roberta (Bertie), and me to finish the project.

We are deeply indebted to Alison Wearing. Not only is Alison a brilliant author and teacher, she is a tremendously generous human being. She has selflessly given her time and energy to nurture us and see this book through to completion. Without Alison's loving guidance, this book would not be what it is. All who encounter her are enriched by her bright spirit. She has helped countless people craft their stories through her online class, Memoir Writing Ink. I feel deep gratitude to consider her a friend.

As editor and publishing consultant, Scott Steedman has been our guiding light throughout this project. What a pleasure it has been to work with him. Designer Jennifer Lum skillfully transformed Sam's words into art. If Sam were a bird she would soar through the air with the same comfort, elegance and grace as the crane Jen designed for this book. Sam was very fond of Senya Prescott and would be pleased to know that she proofread the final draft. Jesse Finkelstein at Page Two Books and Joe Jackman generously provided their time and insight in the early stages of the project. They could not have been more pleasant to work with. Carra Simpson held our hands through the distribution process and amused us with stories of her chickens.

Barb Orchard is an angel who entered our lives when Sam's home medical needs were becoming overwhelming. As a personal support worker, Barb not only cared for Sam physically, she nurtured us both. Covid isolation was more bearable with Barb in our bubble.

I did not just marry Sam. I married into the Albert family. They welcomed me with open arms, an abundance of love and more food than I could ever eat. If you have ever been so fortunate as to savour Bertie's chicken soup or enjoy her knishes, you know what heaven tastes like. With kindness and patience, she has overseen the publication of this book. Bertie and I have grown even closer as we have shed tears together in mourning her daughter, my wife.

My biggest acknowledgement is to Sam. She saw the very best in me and, as a result, I strove to be the person she saw me to be. Sam was bright, kind, loving. Always supportive. I often marvel at my good fortune that she chose me. Sam was unflappable even in heart-wrenching situations. During one of her many Covid-era hospital visits, I was not allowed in her room. She was in significant pain so I crashed through the bushes outside her room so we could visit. A nurse entered and was startled to see a dishevelled man with leaves in his hair staring in her window. "Oh," Sam said proudly, "that's my husband. He does that sort of thing."

Sam died in the spring. I planted her grave with her favourite flowers, nasturtiums and sunflowers, and one of her most coveted foods, potatoes. She wasn't able to eat them during her last years, so it seemed right that she be treated to a feast. The sunflowers grew to be so tall and joyful that they made everyone smile as they passed by.

"That's my wife," I wanted to say. "She does that sort of thing."

Daniel Shoag, February 26, 2022

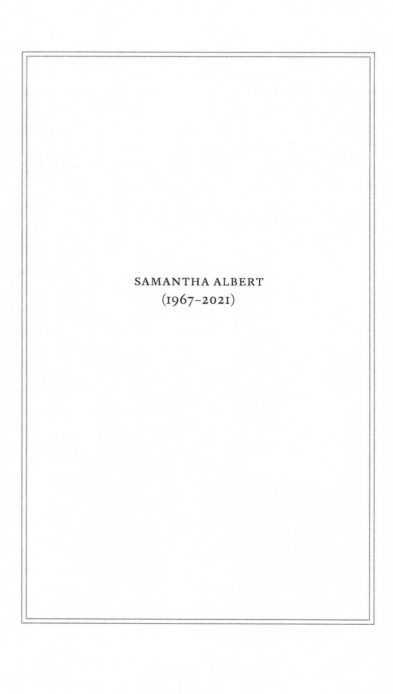

SAMANTHA ALBERT
(1967–2021)

CPSIA information can be obtained
at www.ICGtesting.com
Printed in the USA
LVHW102358170922
728633LV00026B/523